STRONG ENOUGH
to bend

Judith K. Witherow

Twin Spirits Publishing

For information about permission to reproduce written selections or photographs from this book, write the publisher:
Twin Spirits Publishing
P.O. Box 1353
Clinton, MD 20735

Cover Art by Andrea Witherow, 2003

Library of Congress Control Number: 2014933659

ISBN 978-0-9747172-9-6

CONTENTS

INTRODUCTION

Strong Enough to Bend made its first appearance as a drawing. It was given to me as a present by my artist daughter-in-law Andrea. She told me it represented my life, and how no matter what I encountered there always seemed to be the ability to bend without breaking.

I remember thinking, "If you only knew how many times there was the distinct feeling that life was about to uproot me, or at the very least snap off the center portion from which all other limbs sprung forth."

This younger woman saw what many older ones apparently didn't give a second thought. There was always an unspoken assumption that of course I would continue on with life. Whatever was thrown at me would be returned with equal or stronger force.

During the reading of each essay, I was overwhelmed by how many times I should have been down for the count. During the reading of one particularly harsh health essay I asked Sue, "What in the ever loving hell kept me from blowing my brains out?" In all sincerity suicide appeared to be the sanest option. She shook her head, as she remembered countless walks through fire that my mind had erased.

The reason was always the same. A combination of letters that formed a simple four letter word. Love. Love for the woman I've shared my life with for the past thirty eight years. Without her by my side there would not have been the desire to keep pushing myself. Her belief in me caused me to want to see how high I could soar. Apparently no boundary or limit has yet been reached. I am she, and she is me, and we are one. There is also love of our three sons. Love for parents. Love for family and friends. Love so deep the thought of causing them further pain was something I didn't consider for the short or the long run. Whatever I had to deal with was secondary to words spoken and unspoken. What I endured on a continual basis

wasn't something that leaving them could be solved by what seemed to be a selfish act. Not that I ever thought I couldn't be replaced, but in all seriousness there was the belief that no one could or would love them with as much passion as I carried within this body.

I've managed to break numerous bones. Surgeries have been an ongoing part of my life. Incurable auto-immune diseases torture my body and soul night and day. Countless pain filled diseases come and go. Everything leaves scars of the visible and invisible type. Throughout it all love leaves a stronger force to keep me wanting to survive what the present and future holds in store.

Strong Enough to Bend? Only the fierceness of love and survival will write the ending to future stories.

FOUNDATION

- Beginning

- Dwelling

- Habitat

Basis for something
physical or mental.

STRAINED CLASS WINDOWS

"You People." Every time I hear those ignoble words I know it isn't going to be good. They will always cause me to mentally and physically cringe. When these words are heard since birth you know which rung of the ladder you're standing on.

"You People" should have indoor plumbing. How can you stand that outhouse? "You People" need to have electricity and running water. Your house looks so small. How many of "You People" sleep in one bed? (I shared a bed with two sisters, and in the winter our body heat was probably the only thing that kept us from freezing to death). Why don't "You People" paint your house?

Poverty makes you so damned dumb that none of these things ever occurs to you. Someone pointing them out is like a giant wake-up slap on the forehead.

We could have painted any bare wood shack we ever lived in seven different colors, and it wouldn't have changed a thing. People still would have said, "You People" are so gaudy, but that is all the tangible difference it would have made. There would have been less money for food and other survival necessities, but what the hell; it might have made us easier to look at. That's what it is all about isn't it? Looks?

Not the kind of looks where someone is rolling their eyes while they are trying to talk to you. This habit is the twin of "You People," and you just want to haul out a piece of tape and hold their eyes still so they can clearly see what you're saying.

I've worked steadily for the past thirty-five years in the women's movement. I marvel at the serious lack of understanding concerning class and race among many activists. It has yet to be clearly defined or understood by many whom I've assumed should know the answer. I no doubt recognize this lack because of my background. I've taken the time to learn the ways of others and I don't believe it's too much to ask the same be done in return.

For that matter, it's a toss-up whether classism or racism bites the hardest. Most times I can't figure out why those who should know better still use theories to define what should by now be accepted as fact. Reality: Instead of debating these two issues to death, accept the words of those who've always been there. Trust the women who know the answers from harsh experience.

Don't ask me to supply further information when I've written an article to back up my words. Three times in the last year and a half I've been required to supply unnecessary justification for my work because others held prejudice against my class and racial culture. For instance, when I stated the word "squaw" is derogatory to my people, a white editor wouldn't take my word for it. She told me she came from the southwest and had always used the word and no one corrected her. I'll just bet no one had, and she considers herself a feminist without question.

I thought writing this article could be done objectively. However, the deeper old buried familial grief graves become, the angrier and sadder I become. If this weren't so Goddess-awful important, the dirt would be thrown back on. But how will there ever be change unless all sides are truthful?

As a poor, mixed-blood Native American Indian raised in the northern Appalachians, I will invite you into my life and reveal the sights, tastes, smells and life-limiting experiences that were in all honesty not a part of your upbringing.

Despite numerous hardships, I graduated from high school and made my family very proud. In retrospect, it's now obvious I was purposely kept at lower levels even though my grades were always high. No one ever mentioned scholarships or college to me. After graduation I earned a living at various menial jobs. There wasn't the confidence instilled which would allow me to apply for jobs that I definitely was qualified to fill.

I believe you get weeded out of the higher education track at an early age. It's not the grades that count; it's your family's potential that is measured by the class yardstick. ("You People" would just take up a space that could be used by someone really serious about education.) Some very fine minds get lost this way. Yes, you could go to college at a later date, but by then life has had so many whacks at you that it rarely leaves you with the time or confidence to try. Survival often means feeding the belly before the brain. The deprivation of either causes lifelong pain. There is only so much humiliation you can cram into a child before you effectively crowd her out of the system.

My father quit school in the third grade to help raise his brothers and sisters. He was self-educated and gave me an abiding love for the written word. My mother stayed in school until the eighth grade. Her one clothing outfit was the top of a dress for a blouse and the bottom of a man's overcoat for a skirt. She never stopped grieving for her lost chance. She often spoke of her proudest moment as winning a poetry recital before the need to quit school arose.

When my father was in his seventies and dying of cancer, he asked me to cover for him because he had told a nurse a lie. I thought she must have asked him about smoking or drinking. He said, "She asked me how far I had gone in school. I thought fifth grade sounded much better so I told her that. You back me up, kid." I asked him why he didn't just say he had graduated. He looked like someone had pulled a gun on him. "Jesus, girl, you can't say anything like that." I tried to explain that it was a bullshit question, but he was having none of it.

After many years of subjugation you become your own overseer. To this day, I see my nieces and nephews trash each other before the rest of society gets a chance. I understand the dynamic perfectly. If you make fun of or hurt each other, then the second time around it doesn't pain as much. You have already been prepared. When you depersonalize pain and suffering you can ignore it. Only when a human face is superimposed on poverty will this barbaric practice end.

The first house I remember living in contained three small rooms. (The next tenants used it as a chicken coop.) My father had to walk stooped over because the ceilings were about five feet high. He was six feet tall. There was no water or electricity. The creek out back served as washing machine, refrigerator and bathtub.

We never lived in a place that had screen doors or screens in the windows. This allowed everything, including snakes, to come and go at will. We learned at an early age to pound on the floor before getting out of bed. This was so you didn't accidentally step on a rat and get bitten. Why in the hell do rats always overrun the poor? I can tell you it's not for the food. Maybe easier access is the only true explanation.

When it snowed in the mountains, it would drift in through all the cracks that weren't full of paper or rags. We had very few blankets so coats, rugs or clothes helped to keep us warm. The roof had so many holes that we didn't have enough pots or cans to catch all the rain that trickled through. Too bad we didn't have one of those glass ceilings I hear so much about. I'll bet it could have kept us dry, warm and in our place.

This basically describes the houses we grew up in. Each move was a little better than the last. When I was 5 we moved to a house that had electricity. At age 14 we moved to a house that had both water and electricity. We never acquired a place with screens or one that wasn't overrun with rats.   Yes, we set traps. Yes, we put out poison. Many times my brother and I would sit in the basement with a .22 rifle and pick them off when they popped their heads out.

Many times people equate poverty with laziness. We always worked. Dad worked at a sawmill and as a lumberjack. Later on he became a carpenter. He never missed work, and he never received any benefits.

My dad, a good-looking, proud man, came from a long line of alcoholics. My mother sprang from the same background, but only dad succumbed to it. It still follows the male lineage on both sides of the family. Twice while growing up, I heard people use my dad's name as a synonym for "drunk." If the alcohol colored and clouded the ugliness and made life bearable, I can understand and forgive that. Yes, I'm sure the cheap wine he drank took material and mental tolls on all of us, but it was an illness that he fought all of his life.

One time Dad committed himself into an alcohol rehabilitation institution. Mom had to apply for welfare and sign a non-support order that she was told would never be served. It was protocol. (It was the only time she ever applied for benefits). On the day of Dad's release, after two months of treatment, the police came and took him away in handcuffs because of the non-support warrant. On the way home from jail, he stopped and bought a bottle of wine. It caused a breach in my parent's relationship that never healed. None of us had ever been in any trouble with the law. The law was something you feared with all of your being. It still is for my generation in the family.

Mom worked as a housekeeper for several families. I was ashamed of her for doing so. When high school girls whose homes Mom cleaned would tell me in a loud voice at school what a wonderful job Mom did, I wanted to die. On the other hand, to Mom's final day she would brag about what a good job she had done and how pleased her employers were.

She also did waitress and factory work and thought it was a great honor that she had never been fired from any job. Me, I just wanted to shake her when she would start these raps and say, "Of course they didn't fire you. You were the perfect shit-worker to fulfill any boss's dream. You never complained, and you left pieces of your heart and health everywhere you worked." I never said it out loud to her.

She would look at me in total amazement whenever I tried to say that perhaps things weren't as cut and dried as they appeared. She was the kindest woman I have ever known. I will never stop missing her truly honest compassion. If there is a place of rest, hers should be an everlasting one.

Work. That's all we knew from childhood up. You name it, and we sold or did it. We picked and sold strawberries, blackberries, elderberries and blueberries. We sold Rosebud Salve by the gross. Remember those tacky cardboard mottoes that said "HOME SWEET HOME"? Sold them. Countless packs of vegetable seeds were sold door to door. Lawn mowing, gardening, babysitting, etc., etc.

One of the hardest jobs was picking princess pine. It's used to make funeral and Christmas wreaths, etc. It's found growing wild in the wintertime. It looks like wispy little pine trees. You were paid six cents a pound for it. Believe me--it takes more backbreaking work than you can ever imagine to fill a burlap sack to the top. Digging through the snow in search of princess pine without the benefit of gloves or boots is something you wouldn't wish on anyone. We would miss school to help with this effort. Whoever was the youngest at the time would be placed in a hurriedly fashioned lean-to for shelter. Another young one would stay nearby and keep the fire going while the rest of us picked the plants.

Our favorite spot, one where you weren't walking forever to find the pine, was on a state game reserve. One time after picking all day, we dragged our sacks up to the dirt road where Dad was to meet us. Instead of Dad, we were met by a game warden. He made us dump out all of our "piney". He said he had been watching us work all day and he wanted to teach us a lesson. Granddad and the rest of us were afraid, but Mom told us it would be all right.

That night we went back and picked it all up by the light of the moon. Mom said it was too much work picking something growing wild -- something that should be ours for free -- only to have it wasted by someone who didn't know the first thing about nature or survival.

Because of background and lifestyle, our family is riddled with disease and disability. The water we drank wherever we lived came out of mountains that had been strip-mined for coal. This same water flowed down to the river and killed all of the fish and every other living organism.

The town of 400 where we were raised is now full of cancer, multiple sclerosis, lupus and many other diseases. I had melanoma, and needed a section of my right foot removed. I have multiple sclerosis and systemic lupus, as do other members of my family. It is uncommon to have so many cases in such a small region. It's not contagious, so what is the common denominator?

I wish there had been a free lunch program when I was growing up. Health problems like rickets due to malnutrition could have been avoided. When I hear anyone go into a diatribe about all "You People" wanting handouts, I go a bit crazy. The main memory of my childhood is always being hungry. Oh sure, we gardened, hunted and fished, but it was never enough to feed eight or more people at one time. You can't be raised with bottom-line hunger and little or no healthcare and have the expectations of others. You learn to settle at an early age, and it remains with you forever. It's one of life's evilest secrets, and those of my background never forget these well-schooled lessons.

Does society still not get it? An unhealthy child will be an unhealthy adult. A sick, uneducated adult will not be able to work and contribute like a healthy, educated one. This dynamic will cost from the cradle to the coffin if it's not interrupted. Unlimited resources that are now being spent to wage war all over the globe could be redirected to save the same number of people.

My hope is that stories about abject poverty and lack of education will not just be read and forgotten. If more people aren't willing to work to help us change our destiny the loss will soon be insurmountable. If the problems caused by classism and racism aren't worked on continually we will never equally share the benefits of society.

GO YELL IT ON THE MOUNTAIN

At night the mouth of the mountains swallows the sun and spits out flashes of pink and gold between their peaks. It fuses clouds and sky into a mishmash of emotion and stirs up memories long ago forgotten.

Annie and I knew each other for decades, but genuine friendship didn't reach completion until age conjoined our heads and hearts leaving wisdom in its wake. We knew we were more alike than others, but that counted for squat. Anyone can, and does, pass for just about anything. Ain't that rich? More like, ain't it the bar code stamped on the backside of the poor?

We were raised at opposite ends of the Appalachians. Me, from one of the endless mountainside towns that clung to a soot-covered belt buckle up north. Annie reached adulthood amidst southern squalor. Clearly miles are nothing but a measurement if there's someplace to go.

Our families were related in every way except blood. Both of us grew up in a Whoopin' Holler. A Holler is a place where one or two people lays claim to having a phone. If there was news it was shouted from house to house until the rightful person claimed the message.

Even if you didn't want your business common knowledge it couldn't be avoided. The mountains bounced sound around the Holler like a ball against a concrete wall. The shacks lacked insulation against cold, tempers, love making and every other utterance. Laughter always erupted at the surprise folks had when their business became the topic of the day.

When our bond of friendship formed in the later years of life, we instantly recognized similarities. We had a knack of letting our eyes begin to roll, and knowing what was going to be said before sound tripped off the other's tongue. Mocking humor was the binding that held us tighter than twins. It helped nourish a trusted kinship where few ever flourished. Those born into this class recognize each other instantly. Race has nothing to do with the familiarity the "have-nots" are ingrained with from birth.

Annie knew the value of storytellers. She came from the same sorry background that perfected this type of entertainment. During these years of friendship, she always sat front row at my tellin's. When life caved in no detail was spared. If it happened, it happened. What made mountain mockery work was acting out life's drama as if talking about a stranger. Those in the know never needed a program. They would have already spotted themselves.

*****

A train track split the Holler like the well-worn path to our outhouse. It was of little consequence socially. Living on either side of the tracks made scant difference. Everyone was equal in one way or the other or they wouldn't have stayed.

During childhood, my best friend Gertie's family lived in the house closest to the railroad tracks. During one rainy morning she lost seven members of her family to that train and the tracks it clung to. Later I heard adults say the brakes burned out on their car as it skidded down the mountainside. Seeing two of my youngest friends laid out in coffins gave me an abiding respect for a favorite play area.

An alley separated our rented house from Gertie's. Every now and then the county would send someone out with a load of red-dog shale to fill the muddy ruts. This event always beat a local election by a week or two of time. Whatever the reason, it made running barefoot hazardous until cars and trucks crunched and pressed the rock down into the dirt. Cars have always been the dividing line between those who had and the wannabes.

We owned a single seat coupe. Dad removed the back partition so six of us young ones could huddle together in the trunk. If you had a problem about being crowded like canned goods in a jar you kept it to yourself. Whining never changed anything except the riling of someone's temper.

Decades later Annie and I were visiting my parents. A discussion of that car came up. Mom said, "Wasn't that a rumble seat back there, Daniel?" Dad and I just looked at each other and laughed. The sounds I emitted were pure sarcasm. His were from shame at the danger he forced on a bunch of helpless kids. Annie held her piece. She just stared in that knowing way.

The family coupe we'd been discussing met its end in a loud and raucous death. During one of a lifetime of endless drinking episodes, it was rendered useless. Dad insisted he was going to a beer garden in town. Mom said if he left it would be on shank's mare. Dad got in the car and Mom picked up the long handled ax that always lay next to the wood pile. Us younger ones hit the porch like a ball peen hammer ricocheting off a dried hickory nut. She was a tiny woman, about five feet tall, and he was well over six-foot.

With one swift swing she brought the ax down through the windshield shattering it like ice from the first river freeze. "You're not taking the car," she said. He unfolded his frame from the front seat, and proceeded to put his work-booted foot through the driver's side window. After that act, she went around to the front and ax-smashed both headlights.

The sound of a demolition derby filled the night. It brought the neighbors outside for ringside seats on their front porch. We kids agreed that at least our folks weren't shoving each other around.

While Mom was getting her second wind, Dad rounded the car with that long legged stride of his and kicked in the opposite windows. They both stood and looked at the mess they had created. When Dad caught his breath he left on foot for the bar. He would be walking to work, and everywhere else, until a deal to buy another heap was arranged.

He wasn't the only one used to walking. From five years of age it was my job to go with Mom to fetch Dad home from his hangouts. I was second from the oldest in age. If there were a new moonshine still around, he knew the whereabouts immediately.

Mom thought the women working in these places should have some understanding about our poverty, and how many empty mouths were at home. If they had any conscience they'd refuse to serve him. Sweet Jesus on a rag rug, what did that have to do with anything?

These women were just doing a job, and they had the same kind of down-for-the-count life.

To this day I can't walk inside a bar without cringing. You can't forget grown men staring at you every week with narrow-eyed hatred because you were dragging away one of their cronies. School nights were the worst. I knew there would be miles of walking through the snow, rain and cold of those mountains, and scant time for homework or sleep.

What causes adults to do stupid stunts that even a kid can see through? Then again, why do so many kids grow up and repeat the past? Annie says you imitate life. There are no books about child rearing that our kind would spend a train flattened penny buying. She's partially right. I don't drink liquor, and she'll tip up a bottle and suck out the last drop.

Gertie's family and ours would feud over any number of real or imagined slights. It temporarily put a hold on friendship outside of school. Love and laughter ended at the bridge just out of sight of the adults.

We all shared a common trough to catch water. The spout was stuck into the side of a coal-stripped hill. The water was sweet and cold. In the wintertime it froze to a trickle. The beauty inspired numerous stories that helped ease the pain of hands lacking gloves and feet that were bootless.

Many feuds centered on that watering hole. Numerous battles erupted over who put their ten quart bucket under the trough first. Since the water was on our side, Dad would forbid Gertie's family access. They would then have to dip it out of a shallow pool that ran under the road and onto their rental property. The fracas would continue until the women who lugged the water came to an agreement. Waiting until your bucket became full of water was no small matter. When you needed endless amounts to satisfy your family's needs time was precious.

I hated laundry day with a vengeance. It was mind-and-body-crushing labor. All day would be spent fetching two buckets of water at a time. It was too much for children to carry, but carry it we did.

Tote water and chop wood. Keep the fire burning to heat the water. Keep the water steady flowing to wash the clothes. Go to the woods and look for dried out kindling. Drape the clothes over a clothes wire, or spread what wouldn't fit on the grass. Cut poles to prop up the lines so nothing wallowed in the dirt.

The belief that the poor are basically lazy is a mind-mauler. Or its twin, "They could better themselves if they tried." This type of life causes you to be both wise and weary beyond your years. Many of us develop an understanding of others that no amount of time will ever erase, or ease the slack we readily accord kindred spirits who have fallen.

Imagination should have been my given name. At school I was beaten on a regular basis because of the mental escape routes I traveled. These diversions continued through high school. Any excuse brought about humiliation and pain. Often it was from having an adventure book inside a school book. I attended school and graduated because of the books I had loving access to in the libraries.

Many times I wish more attention was paid to English and Math. Then again, travel to places that didn't require an alcoholic behind the wheel wouldn't have happened. Nor would the exciting lives that others led have been accessible. It would have done the most good to read about my kind with a gentler understanding. Our self-hatred was as inbred as some of the folks in the Hollow.

Annie said we are the first to kick our self in the arse the hardest. She thinks the constant need for dishing out low blows and hard knocks should be given more thought. I agree with her belief that numerous little shitepokes get permanently damaged by false impressions.

I always came up with the best means of keeping control and respect by observing life with a keen eye and ear. Imitating those who kept us under their foot with a swaggering step supplied the best mocking entertainment.

Should I be a preacher, teacher, mortician or storekeeper this week? Preacher and mortician I thought. I'd give my siblings and the other kids a double dose of death and damnation. The price of entry to the service was three dead snakes.

Don't ask if any of the snakes I had the kids catch were poisonous. All that mattered was a decent amount of corpses so I could fill the hills with my "Serpent in the Garden of Eden" sermon. This would be followed by a burial adorned with all of the dandelions and violets that could be gathered. Three snakes—no exceptions--or leave and think about your journey to an everlasting burning hell.

Playing school was another favorite pastime. I was as self-righteous as any principal or teacher who ever had access to me. As I dealt out punishment, in my heart I knew it was wrong because of the embarrassed looks my mockery caused.

Annie thought those harsh teaching school methods were screwed up. She asked me where I got such ideas. I was big-eyed surprised that she didn't know the answer. Her theory of whoever said, "No pain, no gain" must have been rich, perverse or both.

She questioned me about playing school and asked, "How could you punish those kids for something they didn't know how to fix? Why do you suppose we took so many beatings?" In all truthfulness I felt we must have been done something to deserve the whippings. When no answer was given she said, "You didn't deserve that treatment and neither did I. It had nothing to do with teaching. We didn't have anyone we could tell, and it wouldn't have mattered if we did. It would just have meant another beating at home for doing something that called attention to ourselves."

Yeah, I was the intelligent one. The smartest, except for that one forever galling instance when my younger brother, Jake, got the best of me. He did it without even trying. It was one of those summer days that you crave like a full stomach. It was so warm it nourished your entire body. Those days were few in the mountains. You learned to guard them like the change you collected from the two cent back bottles others tossed away.

On one inspired day I had the idea to count the tits on a bitch dog that had recently given birth to a litter of puppies. I was about six years old and Jake would have been four. We were busy counting when I happened to see a shadow cover us like a rain cloud. I looked up and there stood Mom with her hands on her hips. "Go cut a switch, Juke." This wasn't open for discussion—nothing was. Usually I would bring back objects that resembled clubs rather than switches. I figured she wouldn't have the heart to hit me with something I could barely lift. This wasn't the time to try one of those fool stunts. If it had to do with sex you better be ready to take your licks. Never mind what your age might be. These lessons were to protect us from those who might try to take advantage sexually. We knew that animals mating and giving birth were a normal part of life. However, it didn't give us the right to touch their private parts anymore than it allowed others to treat us in that same way.

When I came back with the switch Mom and Jake were waiting. He had a puzzled look on his dirty little face. Mom said, "You know you're going to have to take a skutchin' for that stunt, don't you?" I nodded my head yes. There was no use trying to talk my way out of it. "How many teats did you count, Juke?" "Ma'am, there were eight," I said. With that reply I got eight sharp whacks across my skinny legs and back. It wasn't in my nature to cry. It still takes a lot to cause a tear to fall. She then turned to Jake and asked the same question. Without hesitation he said, "I counted two, Mommy." Only counted two? That lying little heathen! She kept her bargain and he got two short whacks.

One day when Annie and me were story telling. I mentioned how betrayed I felt about the dog incident that happened years earlier. "Juke, listen to yourself. Did it ever occur to you that your little brother couldn't count?" In all of these years it hadn't. Her understanding of human nature truly outweighed my keen sense of imagination and morality. No wonder I loved and respected her so much. It almost made up for me not thinking to say the same number.

The story took me backwards through time to another incident of recollection. I was hanging around outside, listening to the grown-ups talk when the air filled with road dust. Good. Something was going to happen and take their minds off my perceived trouble-making ways.

Dad pulled the car up close to the house. There was a huge

roll of something green tied atop the roof. Neighbors began falling out front and back doors to catch a peek. He strutted around to the one side and began to untie the rope securing his trussed-up-like-a-hog load.

"Give me a hand, Juke," he said. He didn't need to ask twice. I was already straddling this wondrous mountain. He winked at me in that way he always did when the two of us were up to something. "What is it Dad? Where'd you get it? Where are we going to put it?" "Damn, girl, does your mouth ever stop long enough to take a breath of air?" He motioned to keep my voice down because he wanted to surprise Mom.

Later on I heard the name of the man who gave us the linoleum. The same man who owned our house, the one who sold us over-priced groceries from his store, and owned the bar where Dad drank, gave us the flooring. Workmen removed the old linoleum from the barroom floor. The owner was going to have it hauled away, but Dad asked if he could have it instead. (He no doubt saved money because Dad took it away for free.)

Mom heard our voices and stepped outside to view the commotion. I remember the sad look covering her face from forehead to chin. "Well, Daniel," she said, "I guess you'll be feeling at home no matter which place you plant your feet."

Why did she always have to ruin the happiest of moments? In my head the words "shudup, shudup" piled high like garbage in the dump out back. "Look, Mom," he said. "Don't tell me we can't use this to cover up the splintered wood floors in the kitchen and some of the other rooms."

As the person who ended up with a rag full of splinters every time she scrubbed the floor, I knew this was a blessing. It would cover many of the spaces in the floor that let in cold air, snow and dirt.

Maybe she had to admit that what he was saying was the truth, but she would never vocally welcome anything that caused her so much heartache. In the end she helped lay and cut the linoleum. I knew she couldn't wait to show it off to the neighbor women, but Dad would not be present when her bragging rights were spoken.

Me? I just wanted to get everyone out of the way so I could splash a bucket of sudsy water around. It would be my skating rink, and I could run and slide around it until all traces of those drunkards were erased.

Annie said she could understand Mom's pain. That it must have torn her heart up to want and hate something so bad at the same time. You do whatever you have to when there are young'ns to look out for.

As was our way when Annie visited, I'd rattle off numerous subjects and she'd sort them out. We were sitting on my porch swing when the discussion of incest came up. She was listening to me rant about the conspiracy of silence surrounding this particular subject.

"Hell!" I said. "The first thing one of my aunts asked after my dad's death was, "Honey, did your daddy ever have his way with any of you girls?" Have his way? NO! But, what if he had? Why did she wait until after he was dead to ask this question? Fear. So much fear that this decent God-blessing woman would hold her tongue except when she prayed for the safety of the little ones. What a horrible fear to hold inside you for decades and not be able to speak it aloud.

Annie wasn't surprised by anything I told her. When I finished with some of my family history she took over with hers. She spoke of being in the hospital having one of her many babies, and coming home to find that her husband had brutally molested their four-year-old son.

She said, "I was ignorant enough to tell my mother-in-law what he had done, and all she said was, 'You best keep quiet and forget it happened.' Forget it happened? It may have been their way for generations, but it weren't mine. I saved my change and watched for a chance to bring the kids up North and start over. What did his momma know anyway? Her entire family gang banged her from the time she was eight years old."

"Juke, it's like you being a lesbian. Some folks are going to think you're the worst kind of pervert. To me it's the way you were born. Lots of folk want to make it out to be something you could stop if you were inclined. These same folks lie down with their kin and see it as normal. They're just following generations of family tradition."

With eyes blazing, I told her not to dare go there again. That not even she had enough muscle to lift that baggage. My lifestyle was not to be mentioned in the same breath with those incest-practicing freaks. She shrugged her shoulders and continued swinging. She would let me rant until my system was cleansed.

My woman loving lifestyle was something she always accepted. It was open knowledge to her from the beginning of the friendship that followed Annie's move northward. The "coming out" didn't stop her from warning me often that hatred lived in places other than a Whoopin' Holler.

Annie washed in and out of my life on an irregular basis. She always dropped by unannounced and would pick up where we had left off. Her memory never ceased to amaze me. I assumed she saved all the clutter-space for her trailer and car.

One summer day she blew in like a tornado leaving the screen door to swing in the breeze. We sat down in the living room where I was working on a story. We started talking about things that happened since we last saw each other. The conversation continued along our usual route, but something was not quite right.

"Juke, you know how everyone said my dad was dead? Well, he ain't, and neither is my sister. I passed her down in the country where the road splits. By the time I turned around to find her she was nowhere to be seen."

One minute she was my closer-than-a-sister friend, and the next Annie was spewing words that made no sense.

NO, and no again. "Yes," was what I said, to buy thinking time. "You want to hear something else? Daddy has everyone in his apartment building pregnant." With this last statement she laughed uproariously.

Please don't let this be happening I silently prayed. It was like a death but Annie's body was alive and moving. The important thing, her mind, had gone somewhere far away. This was something my imagination couldn't cope with.

"Annie, why don't I fix us some lunch," I asked. "No, she said. Don't you know it's all been poisoned? Listen Kid, I've got to get going. I have to take them somewhere."

When I asked her who "They" were, she looked at me like I was one of the demons in her head. She seemed frantic to get away, and said if she waited any longer her means of escape would be blocked.

After she left, I sat and rocked myself and bawled like a baby. Night crept up without notice. At some point the phone rang, but I couldn't move my stiffened bones to answer. Let the machine catch the conversation, I thought.

"Juke, are you there Juke? Pick up the phone." I was on my way to snatch it up when I heard Annie say she was in the state mental hospital. They wouldn't let her out. She could only be discharged if someone signed release papers. "Please, Juke, it's Annie calling." In my heart of hearts I now knew the only hope Annie had was going to come from being diagnosed and treated for whatever caused this breakdown.

Annie? How could you have sit still long enough to let "Them" catch someone so wise? You were always the one with the common sense. No one in my life except you has ever been able to rationalize and explain things without heaping judgment. I don't know what to do. What if I sign the release papers and you hurt yourself or others?

Damn it, Annie, tell me what to do! Tell your Juke how to handle those demons. How was it you slipped into that imaginary area? It's the complete opposite of our forever sister place? Who are the know-nothing strangers taking over the unwritten space in your head? I screamed like a woman in labor. With callused hands clasped tightly to my ears I slid to the floor. This act stifled the sound of her voice, as shock and reality became one.

NATIVE AMERICAN MOTHER

Several months ago I saw an article in the newspaper about a Mother of the Year contest. Fantastic, I thought! Here's my chance to make up for a whole lot of things. Simple, too, because I always believed I had the best mother in the world. After reading the necessary qualifications, I found that not one of them applied to her. This woman that I have always loved was a complete failure according to these printed rules:

"First: She must be a successful mother as evidenced by the character and the achievements of her children. Second: She is an active member of a religious body. Third: She must embody those traits highly regarded in mothers: cheerfulness, courage, patience, affection, kindness, understanding, a good homemaking ability. Fourth: She must exemplify in her life and her conduct the precepts of the golden rule. Fifth: She will have a sense of responsibility in civic affairs and be active in service for public benefit. Sixth: She must be qualified to represent the Mother of the Year in all responsibilities attached to her role as national mother, if selected."

Where did the promoters of this contest find their yardstick for measuring a woman's worth? Was it the same measure that has always stipulated that this is a one-culture country and either you assimilate or pay the consequences? Why must everything be based on white, middle-class standards? I keep asking myself these questions, but apparently there are no readily acceptable answers. What I know for sure is that we as a people no longer wish to deny our Native American background-- not when we see the alternatives that serve as a replacement. Not being able to enter my mother in this contest may seen of small importance, but it's just another in a long list of ways to discriminate. I would like to give another version of what is and what isn't important in a mother.

First, that she be a successful mother as evidenced by the character and the achievements of her children. I can only presume this means college-educated or outstanding in some other "reputable" field of endeavor. This first qualification is wrong for many reasons. The sole responsibility for the character and achievement of the children is placed on the mother. The role of the father, or another male figure, is of no apparent significance. Outside influences of peers and society are totally ignored. What bothers me the most is that it's only the finished product that matters. What the mother may have had to sacrifice in raising her children is of no relevance. She can only attain the status of successful mother through the achievements of others.

Suppose, in your culture, that the emphasis was placed on your ability to live off the land. Just surviving would be a great achievement. Anyone who is aware of the soci-economic condition of Native Americans could attest to this; we have the worst conditions of any race. In my family we are all highly skilled in ways pertaining to our natural background. I am proud to be considered an expert markswoman. I also fish and hunt. My skills rival anyone I know. These achievements are of great importance in maintaining our culture. Society does not view these traits as such. They are considered leisure activities, or at worst, barbaric practices. It is not taken into account that a segment of this society still lives off the land. Fishing and hunting are natural means of survival although man's continued interference with the environment will soon destroy even this option.

What is so wrong in preferring meat that has not been shot full of hormones or antibiotics? It doesn't take an expert to figure that this is the reason that germs are becoming resistant. Where is the cruelness in giving a wild animal an even chance when you are hunting? Is either of these things taken into consideration in your slaughterhouses? We have a natural respect for all living things. It is not wrong to use anything the Earth Mother has provided for you. Keeping nature in balance is something that we have always recognized. It is why the present belief system has all of the natural forces at odds with the way it was in the beginning. These things, I believe, constitute character. Would a contest judge agree?

Second, that she is an active member of a religious body. At face value, this would seem to mean your standard organized church. Culture aside, we all know what role we as women have been allowed to play in any church. This country has always been big on pushing

Christianity. It has gotten the United States a foothold in just about every country in the world. There has always been an overwhelming project to Americanize and Christianize. The terrible thing is that it works so well. You are given religion, and in turn you lose your identity and your culture. This new religion gives a false sense of being accepted. In reality, it is another ploy on the road to assimilation. What you believe in would not be considered an acceptable religion. It would not be respected that you were in awe of the moon, the sun, the earth, and all of its elements. Nor would the Earth Mother, or any other deity, be acceptable in this land where a white, male God reigns supreme.

Third, that she embodies those traits highly regarded in mothers: courage, cheerfulness, patience, affection, kindness, understanding, and a good homemaking ability. These are highly commendable traits, but they won't "put meat on the table." My memories are of a woman carrying water from a creek to wash clothes by hand; a woman constantly in search of dead trees to chop up for firewood; a woman wise in the use of teas and herbs, because unless it was an emergency, doctors were an unaffordable luxury. Superstition played a large part in some of the cures. Two examples: If you stepped on a nail, you greased it and put it above the door. If the evil spirits came in they would slip back out. The wound was also treated with poultices so you were doubly protected. Another cure was for whooping cough. When Mother was a baby, her brother came down with this disease. Her parent's were afraid that if she caught it she would die. A neighbor brought his black stallion over, and had it blow its breath in her face. She's never caught the disease. I have no explanation. I only know that it worked. I know that willow bark is good for curing headaches. (It is what aspirin is derived from.) I know society sneers at cures like these. When we see things like DES, Flagyl Thalidomide and many other things, we can't help but wonder whose ways are really uncivilized.

Without question she had most of the traits mentioned earlier-- courage, patience, etc. If you can raise six children to adulthood, under the worst of conditions, whether you did it cheerfully or not is of little importance. When you don't have running water or electricity in your house, you can bet you don't have much else either. Being a good homemaker in the shacks we grew up in would have been a monumental feat.

Fourth, that she exemplified in her life and her conduct the precepts of the golden rule: "Do unto others as you would have them do unto you." Here she would definitely qualify. She would never deliberately hurt anyone, even when we considered it justifiable. She would make any number of excuses to explain why someone acted a certain way. Perhaps her pride wouldn't allow her to admit that such things as racism and classism existed. The older ones, like my mother, accept it as the natural order of things. My generation is learning to question every aspect of this society. The "golden rule" is one that has to be applied by everyone if it is to be accepted and respected.

Fifth, that she has a sense of responsibility in civic affairs and that she is active in service for public benefit. These two rules stretch the imagination until it snaps. If you are hungry and in rags, civic or public services will not be high on your list of "things to do." Your race alone might exclude you from "responsibility in civic affairs." It happens in the most unlikely places. Having a poor woman volunteer her services would upset the "natural order" even though she would be able to say where those services could really be used. A working woman is doubly discriminated against. In most cases she can't afford to volunteer, and even if she did, getting paid wouldn't be considered necessary.

Sixth, that she be qualified to represent the Mother of the Year in all responsibilities attached to her role as national mother, if selected. How could anyone not tamed and trained in this society's ways ever hope to qualify? I wouldn't want to qualify. It seems to me everyone is too hung up on certificates and credentials.

I would have liked to honor my mother; that is, I would have, until I gave it serious thought. There is no way I would expose her to so much phoniness. She may have been unacceptable in this contest, but in my world she is without comparison

Maybe I haven't expressed all of her attributes properly. Maybe no one else would see them as such, but this business of accepting only one lifestyle as proper is unreal. Somewhere along the way the true values in life have been lost.

COLUMBUS DAY REVISITED

In 1992 I wanted to write something about Columbus Day and the five hundred years of non-stop destruction of my mixed blood Native American ancestry. However, my elderly disabled mother came to live with us, and I had to put the article aside to care for this precious old one.

The story would have been about how my large family is riddled with diseases without number, and how they have passed over to the next two generations. I especially wanted to write about what happens when you are impoverished and live off the polluted land.

We did not have the benefit of electricity or running water in any of the houses we rented until I was in my mid-teens. Our drinking water came from the Appalachian mountains that had been strip-mined for coal. The streams that supplied our needs flowed down to the river and killed the fish and every other living thing. The poisons were so toxic that they will continue to cripple and kill for generations yet unborn.

My mother died on November 24, 1992. She suffered her second heart attack the morning of that date. Luckily, Sue hadn't gone to work yet. She called the rescue squad, and nervously watched for their arrival. I held Mom in my arms, and talked softly to allay her fears and mine. The memory of her hair brushed against my cheek as she told me she felt sick enough to die. Those were just words. I'd heard them spoken before. We all say them when pain or illness seems too much to bear. How could I know that this time she was sincerely telling me good-bye?

I need to write about her. Keeping her alive aids me in wanting to exist without her presence. Don't tell me that she is better off. How could that be without me there to care for her?

She lived for 74 years because I made the medical profession treat her with respect as well as their medicine. It always made me laugh when she told me not to "get huffy" with the doctors. Her fear was that they might hurt her if I made them angry. Just the opposite was true. To quote Audre Lorde, "Your silence will not protect you."

During one office visit her female, primary care doctor said, "You were poor, and yet you brought so many children into this world. Why?" Mom looked like she had been physically hit. Because I didn't want to embarrass her further I spoke softly in her defense. I quietly replied "Whatever would make you think that because someone was poor they would not make love? There is not always money for birth control when you are poor, and it may also run counter to other culture's beliefs. If one parent had to quit school in the third grade, and the other in eighth grade to help raise their sisters and brothers, what do you think they learned about birth control"? An "unexpected" apology was given and accepted.

There has always been a gnawing need to write about how my family of eleven came to live in Maryland in the year of 1964. Columbus Day would be the ironic time to turn our oral history into a written one.

As a World War II veteran, my father received a separation bonus. It took my parents until 1960 to collect it, because of the bureaucracy involved. With the $1,500 allotment they bought a house in the mountains of Pennsylvania.

Having both electricity and running water in the house was pure magic. The idea of flipping a switch or turning on a faucet was something one only dared to dream about.

During the four years we lived in the house various hateful incidents occurred. Our dogs and cats were repeatedly shot or poisoned. One dog was fed ground up glass. It died a horrible death.

Another time a bulldozer came on our land and destroyed my mother's beautiful lilac bush among other things. Putting the ashes outside from the furnace provoked this incident.

A small house fire occurred in the summer of 1964. A faulty pump that drew water up into the house from the well caused it. The firemen destroyed everything they could with their axes. What couldn't be cut, like mattresses or living room furniture, was soaked with water.

I remember Dad taking one of the firemen back into the

house when the fire was out and asking, "Why? Why?" No answer was ever given.

Late one night before we finished cleaning out the rubble, someone came in and poured gasoline throughout the house. It burned to the ground. A neighbor woman told my mother that she knew who had done it, but couldn't tell because she had to live in the town. Right, she had to live there, but people like us could live anywhere.

Mom, I kept meaning to tell you about that stupid Mother/Daughter Banquet in high school. Even now, if you were still alive, I wouldn't have the heart to tell you why I did what I did. My shame is still that great. When I told you that I had invited a red-haired, white woman to the banquet you just nodded your head. You didn't say a word, but the look on your face spoke volumes. To this day it haunts me. I loved you so much that I couldn't bear the thought of anyone making fun of you. To tell you this I would've had to explain what I found so unacceptable. I couldn't. I can't. It would have been as obvious to me, as it was to you. Discrimination resides in every region. In your head, in your heart, everywhere.

You will take no comfort in hearing that I was wounded when my sons asked me not to use my cane when I came to their school. There were different times they asked me not to wear my hair braided, but I always refused. It's not the same thing, is it? I can't be as good and as forgiving as you always were. The pain is piled so high that we're in danger of burying ourselves until time ceases to exist. It's okay to be angry. It has to occur before change can take place.

Jesus, Mom, remember when one of your sisters brought you home a parachute from the factory she worked at? You made us four girls all the underwear we could use. Unfortunately, girls in junior and senior high school had store bought clothing, and again we were the targets of choice. We didn't mention it because it still wouldn't have changed anything.

Time and again you worked scrubbing floors on your knees and cleaning other people's houses so you could buy me a prom gown. Why couldn't you believe me when I said I didn't want to attend? You assumed it was because I wouldn't have a dress like the others? Wrong, I've always hated dresses It didn't matter that I went to the prom with my cousin. Your tomboy daughter preferred it that way.

That's another thing I didn't talk to you about, or did you know and not want to run the risk of discussing something that would cause another form of discrimination? I'll be forever grateful for the way you loved my partner, Sue, from the beginning. During the sixteen years we have been together you always treated her as you would me. It was love at first sight. Same here. I gave her that yellow prom gown about fifteen years ago. She is definitely someone who knows how to wear a fancy dress.

You two never had a disagreement or a harsh word. I guess you Libras just naturally stuck together. I see all the qualities that I admired in you mirrored in her. She keeps me centered when life tosses me about.

It always caused me to smile when I heard you say, "It's almost time for our Susie to be home." All triangles of love and respect should be shaped like ours.

During the last day at the emergency room, I took care of you like any mother would a beloved child. For some time our roles had been reversing, and with the changing of your diaper it was completed. I wanted no one to touch you who didn't understand your true worth.

With my sisters and brothers looking on, I declined each medical suggestion. "No, no chest compression." I said no to a request to do electric shock with paddles to the heart. Even seeing the pleading eyes of my family, I had to say no.

They didn't know all of the battles you and I had fought and won these past years. They still live in a world where you don't question authority. If there were more miracles to be had, they assumed I would produce them. I would have done anything to keep you alive. Anything but let them prolong or add to your suffering for monetary gain. Causing senseless pain to you was more than I could have endured.

Mom, I saw to it that your Living Will was enforced. Your last requests were abided by and honored. Whatever did you and Dad see in me that made you both think I could do the hellish impossible?

When you died I was able to cry. Before that I could count on one hand the number of times in life I've cried. While you were alive to help absorb the pain, I didn't need to cry. Now, I know that it will be a long time before my eyes are dry.

I sleep with your pillow, Mom, and bury my face in it as if it were your breasts. Don't laugh, but I also kept your "little old ladies" talcum powder. I open it when days are particularly long and inhale the comfort no one else can give. What happened? I don't understand this. You always recovered. You always came home. Each morning when I awake I'm happy. Then I remember you died, and my breath won't allow my lungs to expand.

There is just one more thing. I will never again let Columbus Day pass without notice. You, and Dad, will be proud.

CARDBOARD COFFIN

There isn't a day the memory of someone I loved and lost doesn't claw at my being in an unguarded moment. Sometimes I find myself laughing softly about past events shared. More often, the pain is so raw, its physical intensity causes me to stifle sounds that only an animal would recognize.

On December 2, 2004, my younger sister, Josie, died suddenly at the age of fifty-six. Doctors were rarely a choice. With Josie they weren't used except for the birth of a baby. She didn't have insurance, and according to the state, she was too "rich" to qualify for Medicaid.

Josie's death certificate reads like a shopping list of curable diseases. Curable, if money is available for the medical establishment to provide continuing treatment. This represents an insurmountable obstacle for many.

The night Josie was found unconscious; an ambulance was phoned to transport her to the closest hospital. It was a small hospital unequipped to deal with someone in cardiac arrest. The hospital personnel spent the night calling larger hospitals to have her admitted to their ICU. Each said they had no space, and to call another hospital. It's amazing how fast intensive care units fill to capacity when they learn the patient is without insurance and has life threatening illnesses.

My sister had one of the most tragic lives I could ever write about. To know that she died like she lived is more then I care to put on paper, but two incidents come to mind.

As an older sibling I looked out for her from the time she was born. The sister who now sits and relives childhood incidents from the past: One day we were sitting on the rough-cut steps leading upstairs. Josie was six years old, and I was ten. For some reason she asked what I would buy when we were grown and rich. Being anything but gut-sucking poor never occurred to me. I couldn't answer the question, but the memory of the smile on her childish round face still haunts me.

She said, "I do! I'm going to buy all the cans of chicken

noodle soup in the world and eat every bite!" With a hug around my neck she followed it with, "And, I'm going to share it all with you."

Years later we bought a house that had electricity and running water. One winter night Josie woke me to go downstairs with her. I was fourteen and she was ten years old. She wanted me to sit on the steps and share a can of cold spinach. I whispered I wasn't hungry and gave her the greens.

It borders on unbearable that later in life when there was enough food, she became too sick to eat. I pray the Spirits have her plate heaped high, and there's a kind smile on their faces when they remember Josie walking that dirt road with legs bowed because of rickets.

Seated between my oldest sister and brother in the funeral home, I saw our beat-down life flash before my eyes. I'm now the one inventing how much kinder Josie's death will be than her life was.

I tried to look at Josie's precious face while blocking the view of the cardboard coffin that held her until the cremation took place. Why didn't we think to drape that brown box with a blanket? Why wasn't there insurance money for the burial she deserved? Why did those of us who could spare some money have trouble coming up with enough for the price of her cremation and the use of a room to lay her out so we could see her one last time? (It didn't take long for the funeral director to see that pushing anything expensive on us would be a waste of time and commission.)

No one spoke because words couldn't push past the lump stuck in our throat. So many things needed to be said, but no one was brave enough to try emitting a sound that would break the barrier holding back a massive wail of sorrow.

None of that proper stuff we see so often at funerals on television where everyone quietly accepts the death of a loved one. Proper! Proper? What in the hell is proper about the loss of someone you've loved more than life? When material possessions were never a part of your life— flesh is what holds everything together.

I looked around to see if we'd sufficiently "imitated" other funerals. There was enough money scraped together to buy a book for visitors to sign, and the memorial cards almost made it until the end of the first showing. Thank you notes would have to be bought at the store. At this point my memory went blank, and I was drawn back to what brought us to this dreaded place.

Family members, without number, made sure everyone had "decent" clothes to wear to show how we respected the recent loss of a loved one. (We've learned that going through each other's closets is a major part of the death ritual.)

When I knelt beside Sis one last time I took care not to damage the cardboard container holding her beautiful being. What irony. When she was born she either slept in a small box or a dresser drawer. Fifty six years of non-stop work should have earned her a better send off.

As I kissed Josie goodbye I didn't give a thought to the tears silently falling on her and that disposable coffin.

Stifled sobs. Cardboard coffins. Poverty never allows you to forget that anything more might be considered as passing for something you weren't meant to be—even in death.

TOO SOON, SISTER

Poverty kills those it touches
neither quickly nor stealthily.
Sounding a warning would
set off bells of an unrecognizable
kindness that might cause
some to seek help where little exists.

Rather it gnaws away at health,
spirit, and the will to live.
Loss of hope signifies
that you are in the final stages
of what has always been a harsh life.
The wake begins for your death
before those who love you are aware.

COMING OUT

I'm working my way up
from the earthen cellar.

The poor have dirt floors
money gains a basements.

Down here cobwebs and
coal dust cover my life.

Rats and mice flee as I
hop-skip their tunnels.

Amber beer bottles reflect
and dismiss my presence.

Maybe if I lived in a house
with closets I could escape.

TRUTH BE TOLD

I remember my first published poem.
It was written, read and hurriedly put
away. No reason for anyone to endure
those pain filled words. The number of
decades, months, weeks or days is gone.
It's not kept in the oak cabinet where all
my other works are proudly displayed.
They say "time heals all wounds," but
some things scar so deeply that time will
never repair such forever deep damage.

The second poem published remains
fresh in my memory, but for different
reasons. The first person to view it was
my mother. It seemed like she took forever.
When she was finished she looked
at me intently and said, "Tell me the
truth Juke, do you know all of those words,
or did you find them in the dictionary?"
The second thing she said was, "It's nice,
but it sure doesn't rhyme does it?"
These were two of the best lessons
learned amidst countless bits of prose.

Throughout the years I have consciously
tried not to memorize any of my poems.
I don't know why this is so, and I don't
care to analyze it. It's much to powerful.
I just want to write each, and get it as far
away from memory as possible. To my way
of thinking, poetry is a luxury. It's saved for
quick hot flashes of truth that other forms of
writing would disperse over to wide of an area.
It hurriedly says what I might be tempted to
silently swallow.

ESSENCE

- Lifeblood

- Heart

- Soul

That which defines my same-
sex orientation and gives
importance to loving another

HEART OF HOUSEHOLD

From early childhood I've heard it said that no two snowflakes are alike. Why then are my eyes able to catch and match them all in the night light of your city? I don't want to enjoy the beauty piling up on the windowsill of the apartment. This first snow of the season is for sharing with children.

Is it possible my young ones know it's snowing without me there to tell them? Are their round little faces staring out into the country darkness because they smell the weather change? Is it possible their chests ache like mine? As if they've run for miles sucking in the cold air while tears run freely without freezing?

Those three sons that I gave birth to belong here with me. They belong here with us. Such silence has never encompassed my life. The laughs and cries of children have always shared space with wilderness sounds in my ears. The eyes mirrored in your window are looking frantically for her little ones. For some reason their reflection casts no familiar shadow of warmth.

You place your soft pale hand on my shoulder and gently massage it. I'm afraid to say your name. Once my mouth opens you will hear the howling of a mother wolf whose den has been raided. Your ears won't recognize this wild side of me. The role of mother was one you chose not to fill. How would you react if I were to tell you that each snowflake represented a piece of my heart hitting the pavement?

I stay seated at the table while you stand behind me. You probably think you've said something to upset me. Or that I'm in that place where you have yet to be invited. Neither thought comes close to brushing against the truth. Being here with you fulfills a lifetime of wanting. This love I feel for you happened long before we met. Your life experience doesn't allow belief in such a matter of fact statement.

The Spirits know I speak the truth to you. They were the ones who patiently wove our lives together in childhood to form a generous, warm, colorful blanket. In return I promised to survive the harshness of life. This knowledge of you warmed the places where even a sunbeam failed to penetrate.

Who then has caused me to question my decision to be here with you? Love and desire always precede the ability to speak openly and truthfully. Perhaps fear of losing you caused me to put off discussing the five of us. Overcoming a lifetime of distrust will never be easy. While the "what ifs" clamor for space inside my head, the words refuse to spill their unspoken ache from my lips.

I can't stand watching your city crush and discolor the snow as it falls. It's as ugly as the twin taunting me about the choice I made. Wearied by too much thinking, I turn and bury my face in the roughness of your shirt. It smells of cigarette smoke and wondrous female scents that whisper your name. You kiss the top of my head and pull me closer. This is the answer to so many questions.

With deliberate effort I stand so that more of our bodies are touching. You tease me about how much taller than me you are. My response is always the same, "If I were as tall as I know I am, your doorway and my head would be filled with dents." The room temporarily fills with your easy laugh. The laughter lingers in the air until wanting smothers and replaces all the other emotions.

Our hastily tossed clothes leave a trail that leads to the bedroom. Even the worst tracker could follow the clues scattered about. Time cannot be spared for talking. I want my lips buried so deep in your flesh that no cry can escape. If you should hear something you will think it to be the wildness of wanting.

The phone's non-stop ringing stills our passion long enough for us to discuss whether we should answer it or not. Instinct guides my hand toward the phone. I know it will be for me.

My mother's voice says, "Judith, you better call your house. You said to call if there was an emergency, and I believe this to be one." She keeps telling me to call home. The children had called her and they were all crying. The sense of it fogs my mind and I struggle to fight my way back to reason.

The decision to leave my marriage five days earlier was a calculated gamble. The only family member who knew where to contact me was my mother. She knew if I took the boys with me that I would be giving my husband the excuse he needed. He wouldn't hurt them, but he constantly threatened that if he couldn't have me, no one would. Even so, Mom asked if I had given enough thought to leaving him.

Ten years of lies, ridicule, abuse and going against my nature was more than enough thinking time. Silence had always wrapped and covered my tongue like a closely woven shawl. How could I stay and allow the boys to watch the violence escalate? This decision required no further consideration. It was way past time for thinking and time for action.

The last night of my marriage still seems like some other woman lived through it. Him sitting on the bed slapping a buck knife against his leg. Me pinned down by the blankets and the fear in my gut. He kept saying, "I don't want to kill you but I have to." My silence infuriates him. When I dare speak to say that he is scaring the children, it's the rabbit in the snare response he needs. As his fist arced towards my face I ducked. His fist went through the wall, and I prayed with all of my being that he had broken his hand. The pain was enough to slow him down. Hurting himself was never part of the game.

A vow was made that if the morning found me alive the day would see me gone. Late in the night I placed a call to the one who held my happiness. After listening to my whispered words she told me she would be waiting for me.

In the morning, I got the two oldest boys ready for school. I gave them extra hugs and kisses goodbye. Both of them looked like they hadn't slept much. Their father watched our exchange of affection. He hated the sight of his own children hugging me. Jealousy had eaten away the better part of him when our first son was born.

He had an appointment he couldn't cancel, but some uneasy feeling kept him pacing. Outwardly, I was behaving like every other day; at least I thought so. When he could wait no longer, he mumbled something about seeing me when he got back.

Caution made me wait a while before I started packing. His

leaving might be a trick. He might sneak back to make sure of my whereabouts. When enough time passed, I started throwing belongings into a suitcase. Pictures of the boys, writing material, clothes and my pistol were the only things I remember taking. The youngest, three-year-old son, watched my frantic movements. He didn't say a word. Neither did I. The risk of talking myself out of leaving was too great.

It seemed like the car grew eagle wings and flew to my mother's apartment. We talked for awhile before I asked her to keep my baby until his father came for him. She respected my request not to ask more questions than I was willing to answer. Her face looked as pained as mine must have.

She would keep her grandchild and turn him over to his father. He always called her first when he was checking up on me. Mother took the phone number I slipped into her hand. We both knew she would die before giving it to anyone. That man that I had eloped with held no fear for her. My little one was content with the promise that Mama would see him soon. His grandmother kept him busy while I crept away. Grieving would be swallowed until I reached the safety of the car. The wounds could drain uninterrupted during my drive to your place.

Throughout life tears have seldom left my eyes. Early in life I learned that crying could bring further punishment. It also caused other unwanted things. Once, during my marriage, I forgot those old lessons. A puppy I had bought from the animal shelter became sick. It was having worm fits and every natural remedy I tried failed. For hours I waited for him to come home to take it to the vet. When he came home he found me crying because the puppy had died. Instead of burying the animal he insisted we have sex. Yet another lesson was learned from this white man. Grief dared not be shared unless you were prepared for your pain to cause another one pleasure.

The urgent call from Mother yanked me backward by my braid through a tunnel of scrambled emotions. The little ones were crying. Something was going on. Had my plan of him willingly giving me the children worked? He didn't want them. They were only wanted if keeping them would hurt me. I believed that leaving them behind would insure me getting them without more violence.

When I hung up the phone, I explained to you what was going on. We sait in stunned silence while trying to figure out what our next move should be. One way or the other this night will see me reunited with my children. No doubt existed about that.

I called Mom back and asked her if Dad and one of my brothers would go out to the house with me. Without asking she says they will be waiting for me. She stated her opinion that Sue should stay with her. That is my feeling too. We both knew that her accompanying me wasn't an option. Her presence might provoke the violence that we were both trying to avoid.

My next action was to call the children. The oldest son picks up the phone. I hear his tiny voice say, "Mommy is that you? When are you coming home?" The phone is yanked out of his hand. I hear an alcohol-laced voice warning that I better come get those damned brats. They are driving him crazy. He then proceeds to fake a heart attack, and the three boys start screaming in fear. I calm them as much as possible and tell them Mommy is on her way.

When the phone is hung up, I scream every multiple syllable curse words I've ever heard. The plan had worked, but only a fool would think the fight was over. My insides feel like they have fallen lower than a sunset.

We drive in silence to my parents' place. Dad and my younger brother have their coats on waiting for me. The silence is deeper than the mounds of snow outside. Sue gives me a look that makes me realize she doesn't quite understand the potential of violence I am about to face. Why should she? Our lives were night and day divided. Knowing my mom, she will keep you so busy talking that there will be no time to question what is going on.

On the drive out to the country it becomes obvious that Dad and my brother have been drinking. Why in the hell didn't I notice this before? Was the whole freaking world spinning out of control? They spend the ride arguing about whether Dad loves his younger son less than his older one Red rage boils up inside me, and I want to reach into the front seat and knock their drunken heads together. These are the ones who are supposed to protect my children and me? Instead of raising my voice in anger, I spend the time telling my brother not to leave my side for any reason. Each time he swears to lay down his life for me. Then he goes back to his discussion of who is loved the most.

When we get out of the car I have but one thought in mind. This night will either be the beginning or end of my life. There is no other option. The boys cover me like Kudzu vine. I know the only thing that will ever unwillingly separate us again will be death.

True to his word, my brother stays by my side. Husband tries his best to get me alone but is thwarted at every attempt. We pack as much clothing for the four of us as we have room for in the car. I don't know if I will ever be able to retrieve our other belongings, but it doesn't matter. It wasn't like I didn't know poverty intimately. Being poor held no fear. Being trapped in a wall to wall carpeted prison was the place where my nightmares dug in and wrapped around every fiber.

For once his words have no effect on me. All the sentences ran together like a muddy watercolor painting. When words fail, he turns on the tears. Turn them on, turn them off. Fill up a space deep enough to drown in. She who runs With the Wind has filled her lungs with courage and won't be slowed by anything.

Watching the events that are taking place sobers up both of my relatives. The boys and I climb into the back seat of Dad's car after we finish packing. I say a silent prayer of thanks and hope that our ride will be a safe one. The children chatter away about everything that comes into their precious little heads. They verbalize what the happiness of our being back together means. I am so overwhelmed with emotion that new words will have to be invented when I describe the events to Sue.

Our return is quicker than Mom and you had envisioned. You both look surprised as we open the apartment door. How much time does visiting hell and its devil require? Not the eternity any of us thought it would take.

We load our belongings in my car and say our good-byes.

Everyone exchanges kisses and embraces. No one doubts that there
will be further trouble, but for now we rejoice at being together and
safe.

The apartment building you live in is for adults only. While we
stand outside, you go into the building to see if anyone is at the desk.
In a little while, you motion for us to hurry and come inside. We run
quietly to the elevator and get in. The boys are giggling as if we are on
a great adventure. They know next to nothing about city life and the
buildings that others call home.

On the ride up to your floor the children cling to me. You look
over at us and recite: "Give me your tired, your poor, your huddled
masses yearning to breathe free." These are the words I need to hear.
You also see us as the family I've always envisioned. The smile on my
face is so wide that I fear I might not be able to fit through the alien
elevator doors.

ARE WE THERE YET?

Not long ago I was sitting on the front steps thinking about life. The porch has chairs and a swing, but I'm always more comfortable when the earth is at eye level. My partner, Sue, was watering the yard and doing basic weed, seed and feed stuff while I observed each movement her body made.

As a random thought, I asked her if the neighbors imagined we were queer. I knew the answer seconds before her tongue and brain formed the reply. The Spirits know I've seen the writing on the eyes throughout my lifetime. Experience has also taught me that any sentence beginning with a high pitched "Judith" will not be good.

While contemplating a reply, she ran her dirt-covered fingers through her short hair. "Judith, think about it. Two women have lived in the same house for the past sixteen years. Nothing but women's meetings and parties take place there. Neither woman is ever seen dating a man. Do you honestly believe that the neighbors think one is a lesbian, and the other one is her straight friend? Wait a second. You think because you wear your hair in a long braid, and have three kids, that the neighbors assume you're hetero? Admit it."

Admit it? I don't think so. How could she be so dead-on mind reading accurate? It had to be more than our twenty years of living and loving together. Could she have developed my ability to suspend belief and spider spin fantasy?

Fantasy. What a feather soft word. It can erase or add any event to my life with a mere thought. Didn't it inspire the "want to" in me long before we met? Sue was always my lover. When she was first introduced to me, I wanted to say, "We've already met," but I didn't. I remember being very articulate and restrained. That was some other Judith babbling on about the weather. That same athletic woman who managed to drop a bottle of beer on her foot. She was pathetic.

It was hard to avoid being smug when reality and fantasy blended so perfectly. Curly wild hair. Hair that would have made Janis Joplin's look as straight as mine. Tough. Sue taught self-defense, and rode a huge motorcycle. When that other Judith mentioned something about having a small Honda, the room turned soundproof waiting for the punch line. It was the perfect moment for me to adjust my breasts and steer the conversation in a totally different direction.

There were so many things I instantly loved about her. So many that they couldn't be put into spoken word. I didn't want to scare her away by saying how perfect I thought she was. If she knew, perhaps she would think she deserved someone better than me. If I had seen beyond my fantasy I would have known that Sue was not exactly the same as her outward image.

The time was the mid-seventies. During that period everyone was "dressing down," Sue included. In my mind I thought it was amazing that so many poor women were also dykes. Later on I discovered that this was intentional. It had something to do with being secure in yourself. Wasn't that the way? I was finally able to afford clothes that someone else hadn't half worn out, and society up and changed the rules.

We were submerged in different aspects of the lesbian feminist movement. Sue, although six years younger, had more years of activism. I thought she was from my class background, but the exact opposite was true. This was discovered later. Later, as usual, was too late. Race, class and culture were things I wanted completely understood. She was too important to play games with. My life was hers--my real life--if she wanted it.

If there were any books on Lesbian courtship they must have been kept in the back room. My fantasy evolved from magazines, music and movies. After a lifetime of hardship I wanted someone strong to lean on. But I wasn't sure how or if role-playing figured in attracting this dyke of my dreams.

There was a deep need within me to make her proud. To impress her I took her to a turkey shoot. Yes, a turkey shoot. You shoot at bulls-eye targets with a .12 gauge shotgun. I shot against nineteen men and was the winner. The prize was a frozen turkey. It didn't occur to me that guns might not be part of her culture. I was too busy strutting around to notice her reaction. A number of the guys were pissed at losing and tried their best to figure a way to discount my center shot. When it was settled, Sue grabbed and hugged me. She thought besting so many men was great.

Shopping for her birthday that first year is another memory that confounds me. When I was growing up you were lucky if someone even remembered the date. There was no present or cake. Generations of poverty taught you to just be glad you'd survived another year.

What gift do you buy for a T-shirt, ripped-jeans-wearing kind of woman? You take your money, love and lust and head for one of those swank stores. Yeah. Some flimsy, frilly, see-through night thing that you've seen pictured. "Judith, do you recall Sue wearing anything when she goes to bed?" What? I was distracted with my shopping. Did someone say something?

There it was. A some unknown shade of green, girlie gown. Fuzzy stuff was all around the neck and bottom of it. The matching panties had less than enough material to cover her crotch. You Go Girl! This outfit beat a turkey shoot all the way to hell and half the Appalachians.

Everything went fine until I went to the counter to pay. The clerk asked if I was buying it for myself. I should have said yes. Instead, I blushed and mumbled something about a present for my sister. The reply got me the look that the other Judith deserved. Your sister? Geez, Judith, and you were doing so fine in this alien atmosphere.

Looking back over the past twenty years never fails to make me laugh or sigh. How can one woman be so lucky? I am so well loved that the word monogamy is the better part of me.

I'm still looking for that book of dyke definitions. Sue is right when she says that "butch" and "fFemme" are only words. We each have our own strengths and weaknesses, our own likes and dislikes. This doesn't explain her desire to always put on femme costumes for every occasion. I'm just thankful that gene was passed on to one of my brothers, leaving me to choose between jeans or a tux.

The neighbors probably do think we're a queer couple. If they have a problem with our lifestyle, they also have sense enough to keep it to themselves. She thinks she's the realistic one, but I'm the one they've yet to see prancing around in a dress.

I watch as the clouds begin to darken and curdle around the treetops. The rain will soon put an end to her yard work and my backward journey. What would she think if I joined her in the newly mulched flowerbed? The softness and scent of the shredded pine have my thoughts racing. What if . . .

Fantasy, thy name will always be Sue.

NOT JUST MERELY QUEER

I wish this were a story about closets and how you find your way out. The houses I was raised in didn't contain closets. Instead of closets there were cut-down broomsticks wedged into corners. It allowed you and everyone else to view your lack of clothing. Nails were the other option for the hanging of clothes. It wasn't like the walls were being defaced. In fact, covering them with anything was an improvement. We did have a dirt-floor cellar, but "coming out" from that doesn't sound fitting either.

Summertime in the Appalachian Mountains is usually cool at night and warm to hot as the day wears on. It makes you want to spend the morning lying on the porch by the dog so you can absorb and double the warmth. I know for sure that skinny kids who lack clothes and bedcovers need the sun more than others do. Surely that is the explanation for the creation of the solar system.

On just such a morning, I was looking through a magazine while waiting for the thaw out of my bones. It was a magazine some neighbor had given us, or maybe we found it while trash picking. No matter. It contained pictures of famous people. I was about six years old. One page had a picture of Eartha Kitt in a leopard-print, short, tight dress. Spellbinding is the only word to describe the moment. Forty four years have not erased or faded the image of that picture.

It was my earliest memory of a deep and abiding love for another woman. I kept the picture until it was in shreds. Knowing me, I showed it to others while their reaction of shock floated silently away. Don't tell me children can't form deep attachments to someone other than family or friends. My feelings were as genuine then as they are today.

Time has not lessened my early attraction to other women of color. Dinah Washington, Nina Simone, Billie Holiday, and Esther Phillips were just a few of the women who came into my heart via a big-city radio station. My love for them grew out of the words they sang that echoed my life. As a mixed blood American Indian growing up in a white area, I recognized others whose voice and rhythm expressed my alienation. Separating class, culture, sexuality, and race is about as easy as untangling knotted fishing line.

When the far right speaks of children being recruited by that ho-mo-sex-u-al conspiracy, they are not talking about me. Wouldn't I have noticed a stranger passing through the Hollow? If you were to ask me, I'd have to truthfully say I was born this way. To quote my mother, "You were always so different."

Yes, I was different. Throughout life I kept an attitude that clothes didn't mean anything because I was denied the clothes I felt most comfortable wearing when it mattered. As a child I knew how I wanted to dress but I had no control over what was available. I didn't have the knowledge or wardrobe to compete with other girls. Like numerous other helpful items, that genetic piece of information along with stylish clothes must have been given to someone else. There was sparse clothing money and even less understanding for a girl who only wanted to wear jeans and flannel shirts.

For someone who assumed they didn't care about clothes writing this article was a revelation. My life definitely revolved around what I wore. As a young girl, when clothes were necessary to conform they weren't available. Events that required special clothing were always avoided. Constant shame and pain caused me to vow that as an adult I wouldn't care how I dressed. (One exception to this vow was that no one would force me to "dress like a girl.")

In reality, the opposite is true. The importance of clothing covers my life like Kudzu. This truth disturbs me deeply. I never wanted to care about anything so painful in life again. It takes and gives power to those who have even less understanding than I do. Why do your peers think the demeaning remarks they make leave you unscarred? Do they honestly think your intelligence is as barren as your wardrobe? I don't even like to use the word "peer." It makes me feel like I'm trying to pass for something I'm not.

I still wear jeans and shirts, but I've learned how to "accessorize" them to my liking. It's amazing what you can do with belts, western hats, five earrings in each ear, numerous tattoos and all of the American Indian jewelry I once avoided.

When you are mixed blood and queer, you learn to disguise what makes you stand out. From an early age I realized people liked to discriminate knowingly so I developed a closet mentality. Here's one woman who has celebrated more than one coming out since asserting her true identity.

When I entered the sixth grade in 1954, it was an entrance clothed in flannel shirts and jeans. If anyone had a problem with my manner of dress they didn't say it directly. Perhaps happiness closed my eyes and ears to reality. Mom ordered these wondrous clothes from a catalog. If we didn't need up-front cash, we sometimes got new outfits. Mother said she did it to keep me out of my brother's clothes. Never mind that he was younger and his shirt sleeves struck me halfway up my arms and the pants legs hit somewhere between knee and ankle.

I out-played the boys in most of the sports and was always chosen during team play. Wearing a dress and sliding into home plate was not what I cared to do. It also hindered tree and rock climbing and everything else I was interested in doing.

I'd like to think that Mom gave in on the clothing argument because she knew that seventh grade was going to be particularly hard on me. She had to know that wearing dresses or skirts was going to just about kill me. If anyone understood hardship and what the lack of proper dress meant, it had to be her. (She quit school in the eighth grade. Her one outfit was the top of a dress for a blouse and the bottom of a man's wool overcoat for a skirt.)

My sixth grade class picture remains something that still torments me. It was a concession! We all know the definition of that word. You do something loathsome in return for something you really want. To insure the wearing of my new shirt and jeans on picture day, I submitted to mother putting finger curls in my hair. I couldn't shake the curls out because my danged picture was being taken. It would have been proof that I didn't uphold my part of the bargain.

The thought of my first day in seventh grade still makes me cringe. That was not me in female attire. Wearing girls' clothes attracted the boys' attention in a new way. They no longer wanted me to play on their team. It was the beginning of being treated like a sex object and no understanding of what was happening.

My oldest sister was as happy as I was about Mom's decision. This signaled to her that the period of trying to dress us like twins was definitely over. Dressing like me was something she NEVER wanted. She was ultra-feminine, petite, and wanted desperately to fit in with everyone.

When most of your clothes are second or third-hand, it's a challenge to try dressing a couple of your kids as twins. The fact that no one discarded matching outfits in two different sizes didn't deter Mother. I have two theories on why she did this. One, she read a story in a woman's magazine. To her, these trash mags were the gospel on upping your class. Since we didn't have a television and relatives and friends were of the same background, she used these magazines to raise us "properly." Or, two, she thought if she could teach me to dress like my sister I would learn to love it. Wrong. She would have had less trouble putting a dress on one of my brothers.

Twins? When you have children spilling out the cracks in the wood shack walls, could anyone really believe that duplicating us would impress anyone? We could have run around buck-naked with our crotch hair on fire and received the same reaction.

Someone entering puberty can feel and understand the meaning of not fitting in on several levels. Class, race, culture and sexuality, combined with raging hormones, can magnify any flaw that you and society believe exists. Without a doubt, these were the most damaging years of my life.

Seventh grade saw the end of my wearing jeans to school. It was a rule punishable by suspension. The wearing of dresses or skirts remained a wretched task. My sister tried to help me tame my hair with curlers, but it seriously failed. Three of my female cousins also tried to help. They involved me in that female tribal rite of experimenting with makeup. Wanting to wear makeup and dress up came naturally to them. Their ability to apply makeup without the use of a mirror impressed me. It was almost as good as making a double play in baseball. I admired the skill part of it. But most of all I loved them for wanting to protect me and teach me another means of survival.

There were two girl rules in our home. You couldn't date until you were sixteen years old, and you couldn't wear makeup until then. These rules just about killed my older sister. She could be just as determined as I was and didn't follow either "road to hell" threat. The rules were discarded for me. My parents wanted to turn their tomboy into a girl. Why didn't they discuss what they saw as a problem? No adult ever mentioned that the outrageously queer things I did were not acceptable for any number of reasons. My sister still resents the "double" standard she thought existed during our upbringing. Does she still not get it? Her, and most of the straight world.

In the eleventh grade I went to a barbershop and had my hair cut as short as possible. This was in 1961. Sometimes what seems like an inspired idea doesn't turn out the way you expected. The haircut seemed natural to me, but others were appalled. The first day back at school, my male English teacher had me stand and said, "Look how beautiful Judith looks." He took the heat off, and defied anyone to say differently. Given the choice I would have preferred to remain invisible.(For numerous years I decided to wear my hair in a long braid. It was mostly a cultural trait, and I never adjusted to bothering much with hair fixing. I had it cut short again when I was in my fifties. This was after I learned I had to undergo a year of IV chemo to slow down the progression of systemic lupus and multiple sclerosis cells.)

Perhaps when you're as poor as we were no one gives a rat's casket about anything you do. Or they care way too much about things that are purely none of their business. I remember a visiting adult male family member saying, "It's true what they say. A hog always returns to its wallow." He was referring to the beat down poverty of both my parents. No one contradicted him. Marrying someone poor no doubt contributed to his belief of superiority. To this day, 45 years later, this man who married into our family has the attitude that we were put here to serve him. Once in a while I see my aunt stand up to him, but the moments are all too rare. This trap of subservience takes a lifetime of sidestepping. You get used to having your bones rolled like a pair of loaded dice that land any way the other person wants. It snares me more times than I care to admit.

My Cherokee dad thought everything I did was fine. He gloried in my "spunk" and encouraged me to participate in a variety of sports. He and I would sit up late every Friday night and listen to the boxing matches on the radio. On weekends we would listen to the Pittsburgh Pirates baseball games. The rest of my family was not interested in sports of any kind. Dad gave me an everlasting love and understanding of competition. There isn't a sporting event I watch that my first thought isn't to call him for an inspired discussion. I'll always miss sharing this part of my life with him. R.I.P. "Striped Lizard," my father, the Golden Gloves boxer.

Mother didn't understand or care for sports. She was too worn out with everything else to take the time to sit and listen to most things on the radio. I remember her heating "sad" irons on the wood stove while doing our laundry and listening to the Stella Dallas soap opera blaring in the background. The "soaps" were another way she kept in touch with the outside world to help us blend. I believe it's why they remain popular. It fills a need for many women living in isolation.

God, how I hated wash day. It was an endless day of chopping wood and carrying two ten- quart buckets of water at a time. In addition, you had to keep the wood stove stoked for nonstop heating of water. There was fantasy and there was the reality of our life. The magazines and soap operas could only distract and teach you so much. You had to have a vivid imagination to survive what we did. I sincerely hope my mom inhabited as rich a fantasy world as I did. She only had shack after closetless shack to come out of. We could have shared a few survival techniques.

Unlike Mother, I didn't particularly care what the outside world thought about most subjects. While this wasn't always true, I did manage to cover my feelings better than her gentle, tender self could. Since my world revolved around adventure books, thanks to my father, my fantasy escape route was an easier one to navigate.

I cared most about the outside world when it affected a family member. If someone hurt or insulted my brothers or sisters, I whipped ass, no matter whether it was a boy or a girl. Telling my parents was not usually an option because they would question whether one of us had been doing something to deserve the treatment. It was their way of teaching self-censure. This belief never protected them, but they somehow thought it would work for us. It taught me a great deal about self-reliance. This Houdini atmosphere also enabled me to enter and leave invisible closets without so much as the sound of a feather falling.

There was and is a sense of loyalty that time, money, disagreements, or locality can't erase in our family. When your life consists of belly-touching-backbone hunger, and cultural and race discrimination, it creates a bond not understood by someone who hasn't survived the same experiences.

The fact that you live in poverty does not stop you from wanting, loving or having children. Just the opposite is true. I have three adult sons and two grandchildren and wouldn't trade the parenting hardships for anything of a material or monetary nature.

In our immediate family, I was the only female that hunted, fished, and trapped regularly. (Because of numerous health problems fishing is my one remaining outlet.) My knowledge is passed on to the younger ones so that our culture will not be completely lost. They face added discrimination because of these practices.

I'm well aware that many people harbor deep resentment where hunting and guns are concerned. It's a narrow and racist attitude that is applied without consideration to the Native American way of life. I deflect this ignorance and instill pride whenever possible. The increase of Pow-Wows is making my educational job easier. This past winter I had the sons get me two deer hides and the feathers from a wild turkey. It was a present for a "Fancy Dancer" friend to aid in the new outfit he is making. Thus swings open another closet door.

While growing up I fell in love with several friends. They never knew because it was my problem to deal with, and I couldn't bear the loss of their friendship. As a teenager I always chose girls who were totally out of my class. In adulthood I consciously "tried" to do the exact opposite. If I took the class card out of the deck, it would make the game more even.

It came as a shock and puzzlement when white women who had a great deal of money pursued me. To be truthful, it angered and caused me to lose respect for them. Couldn't they see all of the things wrong with me? If high school girls had the power to shake and break my heart untold times, what the hell were these women up to?

I attended no college or any other class since high school. My grammar must have been lacking because it got corrected on a regular basis. The lack of clothes sense I exhibited remained the same. An apt description of myself would have been untamed and untrained. This left me with the conclusion that my looks were all that was important.

One woman took me to her house and showed me all of her name-brand evening gowns and numerous fur coats. (Like I'd know a De La Renta from a blue light special.) At the time it didn't occur to me that she was trying to impress me. I was taught that showing off your belongings was wrong. It also bored the crap out of me. Remember? I loathe dresses. Now there was a woman who had a lot of closets to come out of.

On another day spent with this woman, I needed to go by a friend's house to give her some rockfish. The fish were in a garbage bag. When I took them inside my friend said, "Gee, Judith, it must be nice riding around in a Porsche." All I could think of was, "so that's what a Porsche looks like." Now, I wonder what that woman must have thought of me putting a bag full of fish in her expensive car. What did I know? That's the way I would have carried them in my car. Those fish brought me as much pride, as I'm sure her car did her.

Another woman wanted to buy me a car or put my name on her house. She said by doing this she "would have a hold on me." I never accepted expensive gifts because I didn't want to feel indebted. It had a feeling of slavery to it.

See this is what puzzles me about the upper-class women I've been involved with. Where did this idea of holding someone with material possessions originate? Why not just give something because you want to? Trying to impress someone who is ignorant to the trappings of wealth will be very frustrating. I know if it's manmade it can be taken away in one way or another.

I met my life partner during this period. After a lifetime of living the way everyone else demanded, I decided some happiness of my own was due.

I was also married and living way the hell out in the country. To say I was in a dangerous situation would be to put it mildly. My husband wanted nothing less than death for me. During one of his fits he fired six bullets at me. I didn't know until later that he had loaded the pistol with blanks.

After more violence, it was time to leave, and I moved in with Sue. I couldn't take my children with me that day. Being without the boys was a pain that nothing could lessen. Within a week he willingly gave the boys up. He only wanted them to hold me there. When that didn't work, I received full custody.

Sue was, and is, everything I have always wanted in a partner. When we first met, she was a self-defense instructor and a cab driver. Her face was framed with "gone to hell" curly blond hair. She rode a motorcycle and had killer scars to show from hitting parked cars. Parked cars? I was impressed. I was wowed. I was wrong. Why couldn't it have been wintertime? All bundled up she would have been harder to classify. Make no mistake. I wanted someone from my own class background. There were many problems in my marriage, but classism wasn't one of them.

It was wrong to base my assumptions on Sue's class by the way she dressed or her sparsely furnished apartment. She was dressing down because she had the confidence to do it. What an alien idea! The discovery of her higher education and background came out when it was too late to walk away.

Just recently, while discussing this article with Sue, I stated how much alike we were. "Jesus, Judith," she said. "We're almost nothing alike, except both being female. You live in a western hat, braid your hair, and are totally into your Native American culture. You have a worm ranch in our basement to grow food for the frogs you keep in your bedroom. Then there is the horned toad in another aquarium that only wants fed live food. During your last multiple sclerosis exacerbation, you went outside and killed a rat with your cane." I killed it because it was up inside the bird feeder eating the seeds and scaring the birds. "Your idea of a good time is taking your 9mm pistol to the range and shooting it. Your three grown sons think you are about the toughest thing going." OK. I get the message.

After our discussion, I gave what she said a lot of thought. She's right. We're very different women. Beyond our dress are our conflicts over money. Once you are poor, money loses most of the power I see it holds over the more affluent, including Sue. We struggle with budget and money issues. We've learned to compromise when class clashes occur.

Yes, we're very different women. But I shouldn't feel the need to be like anyone but myself. These are words that I'll probably always repeat to myself. Repeat but not quite believe.

I am different but not alone in my difference. Over New Year's I was showing my friend Deb a really fancy flannel shirt. We share much of the same taste in clothes. I asked her, "Did you ever think you would see a flannel shirt with embroidered flowers on the shoulders that you would want to wear?" She assured me she hadn't. While we were busy looking in my closet, who should appear but Sue. She said that she never thought she would ever hear the two of us discussing clothes. See?

You bet she's right when she says that we are very different. Who has a closet full of dresses and skirts? Which one would rather wear tap shoes than boots? Guess which woman has a sparkly top hat, matching fairy wand, and a glitter-filled baton? Those of us in the know answered correctly. There is really no right or wrong answer. There is also the plea that others will keep an open mind regarding discrimination in all forms.

Not just merely Queer. I'm most sincerely Queer.

I'M READY TO COME OUT NOW

Reaching the age of fifty years was an exciting event for me. Saying the words "half-a-century" out loud gave me more joy than any number of fantasies I could envision. The fact that I didn't believe I would live to this age magnified every emotion.

Most people assume they are going to live and die naturally. Not me. Throughout life disaster or death has always been one short step behind my heels. It nips at them like mutts on a newspaper route. For numerous reasons I picked fifty as my expiration date.

Fifty Years Old! Now what do you do with such a magical age? Anything. Everything. A birthday party? Why not? I always liked attending the parties of others, but never wanted my birthday singled out.

A friend who shares the same birth date helped Sue and I do the planning. We called it the "Scorpio Twins Birthday Bash." There were a few facts that didn't mesh about the "twins" part, but whose birthday was it? What did it matter if we were of a different age, race, class, and culture? We requested that everyone come in costume. Being creative in finding ways to entertain us would be considered a real plus. It might even earn you a certificate unsuitable for framing.

I learned that night, that if it was your party, your wishes could get truly fulfilled. You didn't even have to light the fifty candles--much less keep them burning until you lost a lung blowing them out.

We put the capital "G" in gaudy that night. Sue baked us matching cakes. The dolls she put on top matched in every way but skin tone. Whoever said that feminists don't have a sense of humor isn't blessed with the friends we have. They're probably the same people who would say, "Those were feminists at that free-for-all-event?"

Since time was apparently on my side, I decided to dive into another river of risk. It was now time to talk openly with my three sons about another word. The "Q" one. Don't even start with me. I know better than anyone how long Sue and I have lived together--

almost twenty years. During this time every word but "gay," "lesbian," "queer" and "homosexual" was used. Words like "Mom," "Sue" and "my Mother's friend" were used instead of the ones society would have liked. Try as I half-heartedly might, there was never a good time to discuss our lifestyle. Fear of losing custody, protecting them from bullying and ongoing battling with their schools were enough to keep the words stuck in our throats like bits of triple-day-old dry biscuit.

Make no mistake, they knew what our relationship was, but it was a different time and with each year's passing, it became less important to discuss this subject. Numerous lesbians had lost custody of their children because of lifestyle, but we were now past the risk we didn't want to contemplate. Now that they were older there was no legitimate reason to remain silent.

With end of the year holidays coming, I decided that it was time I had my talk with them. I figured that no matter how it turned out, they would always be able to say, "Remember the Christmas Mom told us all that she was queer?" Now, there's a present you'd play hell guessing or topping.

"Judith, how old are the *boys* now?" Uh, well, let's see. Does it really matter? "Yes. For the benefit of anyone reading about your coming out, I think it does matter." Well, Steve is thirty years old. Leave it alone or I won't volunteer the ages of the other ones. Stacey is twenty-seven and Mark, who lives at home, will be twenty-three. While you are contemplating the length of time it took to discuss my sexual preference, keep in mind that my family invented and perfected the word "dysfunctional". Or, was that President Clinton? "Don't ask. Don't tell."

Without telling Sue, I worked out the words that I was going to say to each son. I wanted to tell each one separately. This would protect them from being embarrassed in front of each other since it was such a personal subject. It would also allow them to express their true emotions and feelings towards me. It was their right. If they were angry with me for waiting so long to discuss this, I knew I deserved their reaction. Dreaded it...but knew I had to take my lash licks.

The oldest son, Steve, was the first one I talked to. He was in a hurry to leave for his home in Pennsylvania, and I was having a hard time starting my prepared speech. As he was going out the door, I asked him to come back. "Mom", he said, "you are going to get me caught in rush hour traffic." I told him what I had to say would only take a minute. (I don't claim the title of storyteller for nothing.)

"Son," I said, "You know how Sue and I have lived together all of these years?" He said, "Yes", as he fidgeted in the hallway outside my bedroom doorway. "Well, do you understand that we are more than just friends?" The next words still rattle around in my head like a pinball before it drops down the slot, and you are left to pony up another quarter. "Mom, I'm not stupid! I've known for a long time." You knew for a long time! I wanted to say. Then why in the hell didn't you tell me and take some stress off, but I was waaaay too relieved. I asked him if he was all right with it and he said, "Yes." He then warned me about the dangers of gay bashing that Sue and I might encounter. He asked that if it should happen would we tell him and his brothers and let them deal with it. I was so proud of him. It was not the way I thought the conversation would go. We had raised him right. My last request before kissing him goodbye was to allow me the opportunity to discuss it with his brothers before they talked among themselves. He agreed.

Happiness misted me like the spray from a waterfall. When the mist evaporated, reality set in. I was now in the irrevocable position of holding two more discussions. Once had been traumatic enough. Why did I have to do everything in triplicate? Stop whining, woman, and get on with it. Keep in mind whose idea it was to have this long overdue discussion.

That evening, Sue and I were working at the computer when Stacey called. He usually calls me every day when he comes home from work. We discuss the events of the day and spread a cover of love to protect us all for another night. I dragged the conversation out longer then usual. When he got ready to say good night, I asked him to hang on a minute; there was something else I needed to talk to him about.

I went into my..."You know how many years Sue and I have

lived together, but do you understand that we are more than just friends," coming out routine. There was complete silence on the other end of the phone. There was also complete open-mouthed amazement on Sue's face. For once, I was the one in the know, blithely scattering words like seed on fresh plowed soil.

"Did you hear what I said, Stacey?" I asked. "Yes, Mom," he replied. "Do you have a problem with it?" I asked. "No," he said. "Do you?" I realized I was rambling on and saying stupid things out of relief, but I couldn't help it. Sue placed her hand on my leg to reassure and encourage me. She could see me trembling before she touched me. We discussed all the reasons why I thought I couldn't be honest with them. Foremost was my unfounded fear of not being able to see the grandchildren he and Andrea had brought into our life.

Before hanging up he warned me about people that would want to hurt us. He told me stories about their other gay friends. They were well aware of the dangers that existed. Like his brother Steve, he made me promise to call if we were ever threatened. They had been worrying for years about our safety. It made me truly regret their shouldering this burden for so long. We said our "Good nights" and "I love you's" and hung up.

Sue, being the gentle spirit that she is, was trying not to cry. She asked me what was going on. I told her that was the second son I had come out to that day, and neither one had a problem with the news. They'd apparently given it as much thought and discussion as we had. She hugged me and told me that this was one of the most touching moments she had ever witnessed.

When I was getting ready for bed, Mark returned home. He came into the bedroom to say goodnight and talk awhile. Earlier, I had asked Sue to please leave the room if he arrived home before bedtime. I wanted to talk privately with him. She agreed that this was the best arrangement. Given the choice I'd have let this talk go to someone else also.

You'd think by now that talking about it would have gotten easier. Just the opposite was true. With each telling I could physically feel my heartbeat change its rhythm. After some small talk, I brought up the SUBJECT of the day. When I was through with the thrice-told tale, he stood and looked at me. He said, "Mom, you and Sue are happy and that's all that matters. I'm just glad we can all talk about it." I told him what I had told his brothers, and that it was up to them if they wanted to tell anyone else. We were as concerned about their safety and happiness as they were ours.

We sat and discussed, for the third time that day, the danger of gay bashing. He too was given assurance that we would turn any perpetrators over to him and his brothers. Not that Sue and I couldn't take care of ourselves, but I knew where they were coming from and appreciated their concern. Who better then guys know what other males are capable of? Their fears were genuine. It had nothing to do with strength. They wanted to make sure if anyone dared to hurt us that they would be involved in our defense. Family members who genuinely love each other take care of one another.

Party number two: Sue and I began to organize a "Dyke the Halls" potluck for the coming New Year. We wanted to tell our friends that we were now officially "out." Friends were coming from Arizona, Massachusetts, West Virginia and New York, and they were going to stay with us. It was going to be one big sleep over. I was trying to keep my stress level stable to prevent health problems from spoiling the fun. Doctors think it sounds sensible when they repeatedly say, "keep stress at a minimum." They should feel what it's like to never know what your health will be like from day to day.

Amidst the organized chaos, Mark came to me with the news that his albino snake was missing. Whitey was about six feet long. The crawling creature had been missing for about a week. This is the kind of news family members should know as soon as it happens. (Kind of like telling others you are gay.)

Whitey was a snake of unknown species. I've seen a lot of snakes, and albino or not, its markings didn't resemble anything I had ever seen. Besides that, it had the ability to rattle its tail. Knowing these facts didn't stop me from holding it and having my picture taken. I did it to prove that I wasn't afraid of snakes. Just thinking about it still makes my pores clench and cave-in. This type of behavior has contributed to the reputation I have...one of the toughest "muthas" going.

Company was coming, and the damn snake was lost somewhere in our three-story house. Sue went to the pet store and bought a caged rat to try and tempt Whitey from his hiding place. We figured hunger would entice him out of whatever wall, closet or drawer he might be hiding in. We both hated rats, but it was his food of choice.

We devised a plan of what would be done if Whitey made an appearance. Our plan was to throw a cover over him, pick him up, and place his sorry hungry butt in with the rat.

I mentioned his disappearance to a few close friends who would be attending the potluck. Without fail, their first question was, "Why did you two allow Mark to get a snake?" Excuse me, but is there an age limit on snake possession? He was almost twenty-three. Surely that was old enough for reptile ownership. Don't nag me. Help me. We'll figure out the age limit later on.

Those in the know were asked to listen for any hysterical outbursts if we hadn't found the snake by potluck night. Anyone hearing the words "I think I saw a pink snake" was asked to get either Sue or me right away. Before getting us she should say, "Your drinking is cut off, and where did you see this pink snake?"

The out-of-town women couldn't believe we hadn't mentioned this occurrence before they arrived. Well, duh, they might not have come had they known. Some friends refused to sleep on mattresses on the floor. I didn't mention that snakes could crawl up anything they wanted to. Their scales are particularly suited for this means of movement. No need to cause a mass exodus and wreck the merriment of food and friends. It's not every year you turn fifty.

Potluck night arrived, but unfortunately Whitey didn't. The rat, meanwhile, was thriving and acting like he was here to stay. The rat was a male with balls like black walnuts before they were dried and peeled.

The party was lively, and everyone was having a good time. This gave me the bold idea of having everyone who had ever had an affair with someone else in the room, to have their picture taken with her. Enough time had passed that no one wanted to inflict insult or injury on each other. That was a real coup. There was a time when some of these women couldn't be in the same room, or state, together.

When the evening got a little quiet, I decided to tell my touching "coming out" story. I had just started telling about the first son's reaction when a friend, Riggin, interrupted. "Judith," she said, "what do you mean you just came out?" I didn't break stride. I kept on with my story. Next came the part about phoning Stacey. Again, she broke in with a pleading question. "Judith, this doesn't make sense. You've always been out." As I looked around the room I noticed other women looking like they had seen a snake or something. What in the hell was wrong with this picture? I'm pouring my guts out and all I am getting in return are looks of doubt and disbelief.

As I neared the end of the story I was now committed to, Riggin made one last comment. "How could they not know you were a lesbian? Don't you own any T-shirts with queer sayings on them?" So *that* was how you did it! You wore a shirt that announced your sexual preference. I knew there had to be a simpler way! With that information in mind, I made Riggin promise to buy me the dykiest T-shirt she could find. I figured that was the least she could do for stepping all over my wrenching story. True to her word, she bought me a shirt that read, "Be All You Can Be--Militant Homosexual." It's a shopping shirt to wear to the "Maul."

As much as I hate to admit it, Sue and I were the only two who were surprised with my gut-grabbing story. The fact we were the only ones with children was no doubt the explanation. Unless you have the young lives of others to protect, you can't begin to fathom the lengths society will demand of you and yours.

1 can't envision another way of doing things other than the way we did. Sue's lack of child rearing experience and my constant medical problems didn't leave us with many options. As it is, I'll always believe that out of constant chaos we created a family the equal of few I've ever known.

I kept telling my lovely yet traumatic story so others could say or think, "Is she putting us on? No one is that dense." That shows how little my family and friends know about me. My one wish was that someone else was telling the story, and I was sitting there listening. Where was that damn snake when you really needed it?

That damn snake made his appearance a month later. I was playing a computer game while Sue was talking on the phone. My dog, Willie, kept barking non-stop and wouldn't listen to my command to cease. It probably meant a family member was knocking at the door. That's just about the only time our two dogs turn into killer sentries. We must not have heard the knocking with the music playing so loudly. Since Sue was on the phone, I got up to check the door. No one was there. I looked back our hallway to tell Willie to stop the noise. He and Sue's dog Jessie were in the bedroom behind a gate. When I turned to hush the dogs, I saw about four feet of snake crawling under the bathroom door. Whitey was now doing his version of coming out. I don't like to use the word "scream" when referring to myself, but that is exactly what I did.

"Whitey's in the house. Whitey's in the house". It sounded like a bad Rap song. "Hang up the phone and help me." Meanwhile, I went into the bathroom to block his escape. Chastise me later with common sense talk about hungry snakes and compromised immune systems. I reached behind the clothes hamper and closed the floor vent. Who knew how much weight he had lost in five weeks? That snake wasn't getting away if I could help it. Yes, the snake's head was also back there. After closing the vent I stepped into the bathtub---effectively closing off my escape route. Mistake number who's counting.

Back in the livingroom, Sue was doing donuts in the middle of the floor. She was screaming, "What's our plan? What were we going to do when we located him?"

Words and sounds that I had only heard in the movie "The Exorcist" came out of my mouth. "Come in here and help me. It's slithering up the wall!" "Okay, Judith, she said, I'm putting on my leather gloves and hooded sweatshirt." Only the Spirits kept me from adding an albino boa to her outfit. We had carefully worked out our retrieval plan weeks earlier because I couldn't risk being bit. Now was not the time to lose our collective memory.

Into our tiny bathroom she came, fully outfitted, and with a huge coverlet to throw over the snake. The cover was useless. It was so thick that she couldn't feel the snake beneath it. I would have departed, but I managed to pull a groin muscle when I stepped into the tub. "Throw a towel over it if you don't think your gloves will protect you," I volunteered between clenched teeth. She chose our best flamingo pink towel. "No way," I said. "Not our good towel!" I was waiting for her to tell me to take over if I knew so much, but she didn't.

Whitey started to climb the wall a second time. That now made three of us. Sue found the snake's shape under the towel, and started working her way; hand over hand, up its rigid body. It was a sight that had to be seen. I'd only seen it done on a baseball bat. When she made it to the head we both gave a huge sigh of relief. It was not happy being held this way. In fact, we had to bend it in half to get it through the doorway.

Sue pleaded with me to come upstairs with her to put it in with the rat. In all fairness, pulled groin or not, I knew I had to go along in case she needed help. Kidding was one thing, but I would never allow anything to harm her if I could prevent it from happening. We accomplished the securing of rat and snake without further incident.

We were in the bedroom congratulating ourselves on what we had done when Mark came home. He listened in awe to our story until we came to the part about putting the two varmints in the same container. "Mom," he said, "Tell me you didn't put two territorial animals together?" Now that he mentioned it I remembered that animals staked out their territory, and woe to anyone violating their space. Whoopsie.

He came back downstairs to tell us that they were both alive. Drinks all around for that remark. Did he sincerely think we cared about the well being of either? He mentioned that Ratman had tried to bite him. Also, the rat was now too big for Whitey to eat. He would need some mice. Does the phrase........ never mind. I strongly suggested that he bring the snake aquarium downstairs so I could check its whereabouts on a regular basis. He wisely chose to do so.

Ratman became Sue's pet. She took over his personal needs, but wisely didn't get too close without her gloves and other paraphernalia. He was moved downstairs, and put in a separate cage.

My fifty-year hatred of rodents remains. I don't care how cute some folks think they are. Sue takes a lot of time arranging his cage. She even bought him an exercise wheel. If there is one thing rats like to do it's exercise. Honey also spends a lot of time wondering why he trashes his home. I could explain why rats have the reputation they do, but it's more entertaining to just sit and watch.

FIFTY YEARS OLD. Don't tell me how good I look. Just marvel as I do that the aging process continues despite the curve balls life keeps throwing my way.

SOUNDS LIKE LOVE

The way you talk
a lilting sound
that causes
each bird to
tilt its tiny head
as if listening for
a favorite food.
What echo
brings everything
in nature to a halt?
It's she who walks
the earth with
clouds cuddled 'round
her slim shoulders.
Crows feet dance upon
the corners of
her eyes as laughter
rolls along the ridgetop.

Judith K. Witherow

AND, OH

There was that time
You didn't see me
watch you twirl wildly
beside the swollen
creek
about to leap with
rain pure intoxication
across banks aching
to embrace you also

Another day you sat
with stiff bowed back
and upraised knees as
if protecting self from
memory
Curly tossed hair covers
the pale face pressed into
trembling hands frozen in
yet another lover's time
And, oh

SHE WALKS

Our moon sparse house
barely catches a glimpse
of comings and goings.
Shadows traced on the
vacant walls leave old
jagged outlines of a life.

Wind brushed trees rustle
leaves against the panes,
scratching a bereft refrain.
Will your body slip between
slivers of darkness and light
shadowing the watchers sight?

The wistful one awaits slight
creaking upon the splintered
boards. Bare feet don't allow
much sound to echo warning
for one held captive by need.
Where've you been again my
Woman?

YOUR REPLY

Such wonder I have never
wanted to share for fear
of laughter or shame in
eyes that love completely

When I whisper the moon
has just about reached
the lushness of a melon
full and dripping nectar.

Or, quick come with me.
Rain has fallen without
cease and has swollen near
to overflowing the bridge.

If I should say the sky will
be showering sparks of gold
upon this mystic half night
will your eyes mirror delight?

Come my eager tame one.
Hurry and lift the feet that
walks upon pavement. I know
where a hive of bees swarm.

You now laughingly follow
When ever nature calls out
my name to share with you
what others might dismiss.

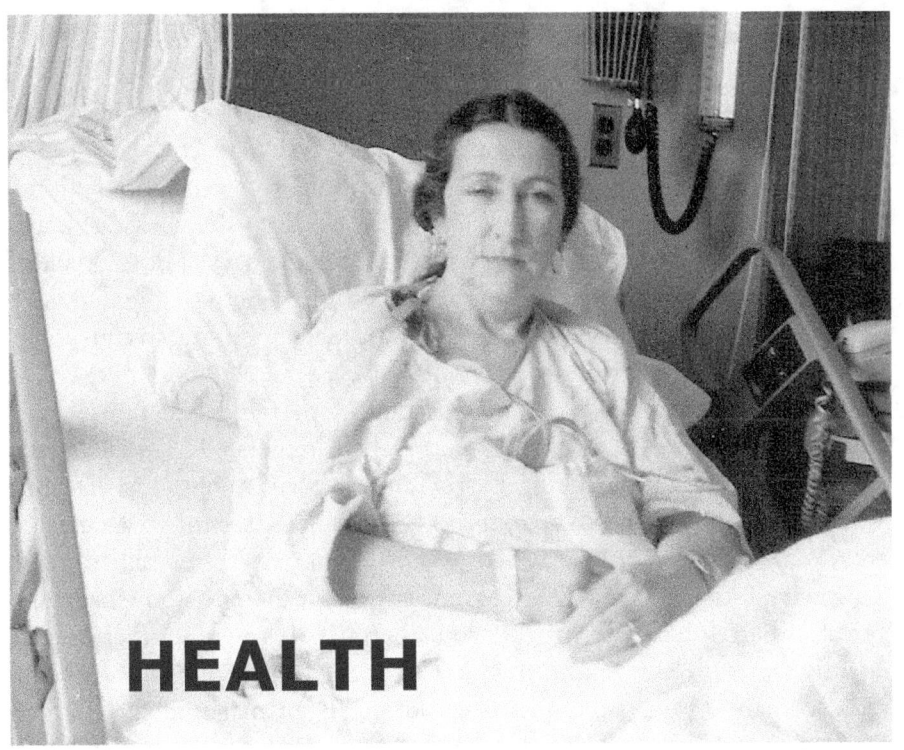

HEALTH

- Status

- Wellbeing

- Debility

The state or condition of
one's body.

WAILING WITH THE WOLVES

The wolves are not outside the door. Over the past few lifetimes, but especially the last two decades, they have crept in one at a time until my house and head are filled with their presence. Sometimes, if the Spirits are in a benevolent mood, I can keep the pack distracted for short shadows of time. The winter causes the days light to quicken, but why didn't anyone give more thought to the length of the nights?

Most mornings I brush past my friends with out so much as a word. It hurts too much to talk. I head for coffee, the computer and a fistful of pills. When we start to howl in perfect pitch unison, the written words drop off my outstretched fingers. The shaky one-syllable-at-a-time outpouring is sometimes worth saving. Just like me. There are times when the paranoia of steroids causes me to accuse the pack of turning on me. When this happens they give each other a knowing look and slink silently away. I shout at them to come back and finish their feasting frenzy. It won't happen. It's just another coping game that we play. We all know they're trying to sort out the confusion of so many muscles tied in sinewy knots. Their magnificent teeth are not equipped to do such painstaking work and neither are mine. It makes it almost impossible to work through clenched teeth.

Many humans have suggested a cure, treatment or theory to aid in my recovery. Thanks, but no thanks. The wolves and I have chosen to rely on each other's wisdom. If the pain of muscle wasting and swollen joints outweighs the fear of yet another unknown we will relinquish some of our control.

Recently, a decision was made to try something different. Massage therapy. It seemed frightening for us to give control to yet another person. This form of treatment wasn't even invasive - other than into privacy - so how could it help? When we arrived at the massage therapist's house she told me to get undressed, and she would be right in. I told the pack to lie under this strange table and pay close attention to what was about to take place. The ruffs on the back of their necks were standing straight up. This was not a good omen. It felt like my short hair was doing the same thing. On surveying the room, we noted that there was a back door. We looked at it, then at each other. It would be all right. This room would not turn into a large box trap if we were prepared.

I was lying on the massage table, lost in thought, when the air suddenly filled with the "cawing" of crows. "What is this?" I said out loud. Crows didn't fly or make that noise at night. It was followed shortly by the sound of splashing waves. There was no body of water of such magnitude in this area. Never mind the thoughts of a massage. Nature was totally out of balance here. When I heard the musical strain of flutes and whales, insight and another culture collided head on. Quiet laughter and low throaty growls filled the room. I tapped on the side of the wooden table to silence my guardians. We would discuss it back in the safety of our own home. So, this was massage therapy. I'd file it away to share with my family. Not that they were as brave as I was. It would be done to impress them.

The therapist entered the room and started asking me questions about my health. I tried to concentrate on what she was saying, but the pack kept interrupting me. They think they know more about my condition than I do. To regain control, and to show proper respect, I told her about my friends under the table. Her eyes narrowed like a fox watching a chicken that has gotten loose from its coop. She must have thought my mind and not my body needed a professional.

Anger at the response that my honesty caused hissed from my lips and pores. Before she had a chance to walk away I said, "If you can't do this my way, then you are of no help to me. Where is your belief in the whales and little chirping birds I've been listening to? Are those sounds coming from your tape player just a distraction, or do you believe they are of benefit to those you massage? I don't know your kind of music. Nor am I familiar with the sounds of the other wildlife. Your knowledge of healing through massage is what brought us here today."

I felt the pack rustling as they got to their feet under the table.

I, too, sat up and started putting my clothes back on. "Wait," the therapist said. "I didn't understand. You and your 'friends' are welcome to stay." We cautiously lay back down as the first massage began.

The next time we returned everyone knew what to expect. We are now at one with the therapist and her way of doing things. It's decided that she be given a copy of wolves howling to add to her collection, and we present it to her.

Many times she asks, "Are you okay Judith? Are you with me?" I have enough trust to tell her, "I'm off running with the pack." Or, "We are curled up in a protective circle. I'm too cold and exhausted to move. Just do what you have to do." Sometimes she asks me to tell her where the pain is. I tell her that the pack will let her know when her hands make contact with a sensitive area. Without fail, when she touches a sore spot the room fills with the sound of mournful howling. The wolves have taken on my pain. Dividing it equally causes less suffering to be felt by all of us.

During one massage the therapist told me that many people would freak at the sound of my wolves. I told her, "Perhaps they shouldn't listen. The magic is undoubtedly too powerful for what's ailing them. Save it for those that your little chirping birds can help." The room filled with a mixture of female laughter and the "yips" of the pack.

One morning, while I was busy writing, the pack started pacing back and forth behind my chair. I finished with what I was doing before giving them my attention. "We need to discuss that tape recording of the crows", the second in command said. "The idea that crows are a source of comfort or healing to anyone is causing us to question how others think. How can anyone revere the black feather garbed morticians of roadkill?" Before he could finish his thought another added, "I've never seen a dead crow in all of my years of hunting. How is it that they attend to death, but escape it themselves?" I asked them if they had ever seen a flock of crows chase an eagle away from something it had killed for itself and its young ones? Several sleek furred heads nodded "yes" at this question. Not just eagles, but animals and birds of all types fall prey to the cunning of the crow. The questions were many. The answers were few. It was agreed that since we knew so little about these creatures that we would pay them closer attention in the future.

Tonight there is a full moon. It will intensify everything. We're headed for the craggy mountaintop. As leader, I'm loping and limping well ahead of the pack. All they see is a flash of my hindquarters as the pain bounces off me in quick, jagged bursts of lightning. This night is mine. I am the alpha wolf. No one but me can touch or tame this night. As I claw upwards, amongst the loosened rocks, I see below countless tribes. The sick, dying and dead cover the ground like a blanket below us.

Some day, when you are stronger, I will tell you secrets that you will swear are so evil that not even a human could conceive of them. Deliberate poisoning of all that we drink, eat, breathe and create. Yes. It's not just me or my family. No. It is not an amazing coincidence that so many relatives have multiple sclerosis, systemic lupus, Parkinson's, sarcoidosis, arthritis, cancer, vitiligo and much, much more. Environmental. Monumental. Generation after generation. This monster is perpetual. It's enough to make the most well-bred, two-legged person howl.

The question of the strength of crows is no longer without answer. What others could not do the evilness of the West Nile virus has accomplished. Whoever unleashed this demonic plague is open to speculation.

I can't end this story without writing about another tragedy. The massage therapist, Peggy, that I wrote about in this story lost her partner of seventeen years at the Pentagon on 9/11. Sheila was a civilian worker, and one of the most peace loving women I have ever had the great pleasure of knowing. Often, life is one dry-eyed cry after another.

HELLO WALLS

HELLO WALLS! That was the hand-lettered poster I had my partner tape above the bed. Not where I could see it, but where anyone else entering my bedroom could view it. It was an act of desperation to call attention to my isolation, fear and loneliness. The sign is down now, but the reasons that led to its creation still exist.

My story begins twenty one years ago when I was diagnosed as having multiple sclerosis (MS). The onset of the disease started years earlier but the diagnosis could not be confirmed until that time. (Today, an MRI, Magnetic Resonance Imaging, can diagnose the disease at a much earlier stage.)

MS is called the "great crippler of young adults" because it usually strikes between the ages of 18 and 40 years old. The disease is more prevalent among women than men for unknown reasons. Researchers have tried for years to determine whether a slow acting virus, heredity or environment causes multiple sclerosis.

It is a disease of the brain and spinal cord (central nervous system). When MS strikes, myelin, the protective coating that covers all nerves, is destroyed and replaced by scar tissue. Impulses which travel along nerves from the brain to various parts of the body allowing you to feed yourself, brush your hair, walk or focus your eyes are short circuited at the scarred areas.

It is not contagious, preventable or a mental illness. It can, however, alter your emotions, causing you to laugh or cry indiscriminately. Some of us are completely paralyzed in addition to having vision, bowel, bladder, speech, or other neurological problems, while others are able to carry on with normal or near-normal activity with periods of incapacity.

On July 23, 1993, the FDA approved the first new drug in twenty-five years for treatment of MS called Interferon Beta 1B. You must have relapsing/remitting MS, and be ambulatory to qualify for the treatment. During the testing, Interferon injections are given every other day and the one side effect noted was flulike symptoms. Scarring of the myelin sheath was also shown to be reversed. There are now several other medicinal options available. The decision to try any of them needs to be discussed with a physician.

Until the Interferon trials no drug had been found to modify in any substantial way the natural course of the disease. Various drugs were tried in an effort to control muscle spasms, tremors, spasticity, etc. Cortisone or corticosteroids are used during an exacerbation to speed healing of the breakdown in the myelin sheath. Their usefulness is of a debatable nature.

There are also individuals using snake venom, bee stings or HBO, (hyperbaric oxygen chambers) to bring about relief or a cure on their own. I've refused all experimental testing so far. (As a Native American, I grew up with more than enough traditional and nontraditional treatments used in the name of a cure).

I have faced some exacerbations with steroids and some without this treatment. The main difference I noticed was the hellish steroidal side effects with the use of this drug. Water retention, mood swings, sleeplessness, hunger, loss of bone density, etc., were a few of the side effects I experienced. Doctors emphasize avoidance of physical and emotional stress, and then they subject you to this type of treatment where controlling your own well being is greatly distorted and impaired.

I have described the diagnosis and prognosis of MS, but learning to cope with an incurable disease is where the real battle begins. Knowing that it is incurable is a burden unto itself. It removes the certainty that with time and medical help you will recover. Many times the disease does go into a period of remission, sometimes for years, months, or weeks giving you a false hope that the doctors were wrong in their diagnosis or that a cure has been achieved.

Throughout my youth I played various team sports, but basketball was the most rewarding. In 1974 I played my last women's softball game, quitting the team because something was happening to my legs. I couldn't run as fast because of muscle strain, and the coordination I so highly prized was deteriorating for no apparent reason.

One of my main interests in life had always been sports. If I couldn't play I would find an outlet along similar lines. They were just starting to allow girls to play Little League baseball with the boys. The treatment the girls received disgusted me. Knowing the league was short-handed in the umpire department, I volunteered. This way I could see that the girls were treated fairly.

I was the first woman umpire in our county. Women who had been my friends turned against me for daring to enter this male stronghold. Every time I walked onto the field I was greeted with "war whoops." The old discrimination was back two-fold. It hurt and angered me, but it opened the door for other women. It also led to my joining the women's movement. It was time to stop fighting alone.

In 1975 I put all of my energy into fighting for the rights of women. The passage of the Equal Rights Amendment became my fight of choice. It was a new and exciting period in my life. There were conferences, organizing, speaking engagements, travel and rallies. Everything was falling into place and my old confidence was back.

The literary side of me that I had always suppressed was beginning to gain recognition. Articles and poetry flowed with little effort. The world was mine.

In January of 1977 my marriage came to a past due end. It would have ended sooner, but with a high school education and three small children to raise, my options were limited. It sometimes seems easier to take the abuse of one man than all of society.

Sue and I began living together. She was an activist in the women's movement. She helped found the D.C. Rape Crisis Center and was a self-defense instructor. We shared a common bond on many of the issues. The children adapted easily to having two mothers.

In March and October of 1977, I underwent major surgeries involving the removal of both ovaries because of endometriosis. December of 1977 found me having a third surgery to repair my urinary tract, and the loss of two thirds of my right kidney because of the previous doctors' negligence. Then in April of 1978, I had a section of my foot removed for melanoma, a form of cancer. These surgeries and other "stressful" situations led to my first MS attack.

It occurred in March of 1979. I awoke from a nap with my entire left side numb from my eye down to my foot. My speech and vision were also affected.

The neurologist I was sent to did numerous tests. In secret he told Sue that all signs pointed to a brain tumor. He thought the previous cancer had spread to my brain and that my chances of survival were slim. I was the one supposedly dying, and I wasn't even accorded the decency of knowing from what or when. Sue, of course, told me so I could put my life in order. She was so used to my calamities that it was just one more stream for us to cross.

As the Spirits would have it, the tests proved negative. They then suspected a stroke, but the doctor refused to discuss it with her or me. No doubt his ego was bruised from the first wrong diagnosis.

A month later another exacerbation occurred. Again I lost the use of my left side, and the previous therapy I had undergone was undone. At this time I changed doctors. After reviewing a number of tests and my case history, he diagnosed me as having MS.

My one complaint to date is that no doctor of any type has ever told me what I could expect. My theory is that if you have a husband for the doctors to discuss your case with, you will get some details. Otherwise, if they tell you the symptoms, you will immediately manifest them with no man to hold you in check. With various medical books and journals, I educated myself. I had everyone bird-dogging for information for me. (Everyone should research his or her illness as a survival mechanism).

Through all the other operations and illnesses I had remained optimistic, but this time no surgery or medicine would heal me. Nothing, just the knowledge of how insidious the disease could be, just that it was incurable. The old athletic me was a wistful thought from the past, but with constant therapy, I learned to walk again.

In the winter of 1979 and early 1980, I had three more attacks. The first one in December struck my right side. I had learned to cope with my weak left side by using a cane to get around. Now, I couldn't even do that. With the help of a therapist who came to our house, I was able to build up the unaffected muscles and could walk again.

When two more exacerbations struck in rapid succession, I went into a deep depression. I decided I didn't want to fight anymore and resigned myself to living out the rest of my life in a wheelchair. Between the side effects of the steroids and never gaining and maintaining any progress, I felt my only option was to give in and save my sanity.

Time passed, and then one morning I had to write an absentee note for one of my sons; I found I was unable to hold a pencil or write. My muscles had atrophied by not using them, and now the one skill of writing that I had retained was lost. That day I promised myself that if I was able to regain the ground lost, that no matter how discouraged I became, I would never give up again.

It hasn't been easy, but others can be of immeasurable help when it comes to maintaining a positive outlook. Support can make a significant difference in your recovery. You have to have a reason to live or fight; everyone needs this.

The hardest part of an illness can be in the way that your mate, family, friends or strangers react or respond to you. All of a sudden you become a freak or someone no longer recognizable. You're still the same person but somehow all that is seen is your disability. People avert their eyes as if they are ashamed that they are still walking around. (Believe me when I say that everyone is temporarily able-bodied).

Please continue to smile when you see us out and about. It won't be misinterpreted as mocking. Don't use a double standard in reacting to a handicapped person; we have the same feelings as anyone else, and we don't want preferential treatment. It's demeaning.

The American Disabilities Act has aided in the removal of many of the man-made obstacles. Many have rejoined the walking world, but the simplest trip takes extensive planning. You need to know if there are steps, elevators, curbs, crowded aisles, parking, bathrooms, etc.

True, we do have a few handicapped parking spaces, but many times these spaces are filled by able-bodied persons. These spaces are wider to make unloading a wheelchair easier and they afford greater visibility. You are very vulnerable when seated low in a chair.

Handicapped license plates or permits are not given without a doctor's certificate, and your application has to be renewed every couple of years. Twice I have had police officers approach me in a handicapped space and tell me "You don't look handicapped". What the hell is a handicapped look?

There's another thing that I hear all the time, "you don't look sick, you look good." Well, gee, that's great. I'd hate to feel so rotten and look bad too. My other favorite, always from men, is "what's a young thing like you doing with a cane?" I want to say, "It's a hook to haul your stupid butt to the ground with," but so far I haven't. I think uncreative lines are their own curse.

You also receive a restricted driver's license because you are deemed unable to judge your capabilities because of your handicap. If anything, we are more careful; we don't need further injury. I think if the Department of Motor Vehicles wanted to be really fair, they should make alcoholics and addicts take their driving test wasted. When they made me retake my test due to disability, they didn't wait for me to get cured.

I want to stay as active as possible, but the sheer nature of MS makes long range commitments difficult. There needs to be an understanding of how to work around limitations imposed. That if I am unable to attend meetings, to allow for input over the phone. Include handicapped women in projects or jobs as you would anyone else, but with the understanding that it might become necessary to do some of the work at home. Or you might have to pull back all together and later on take part in a new program.

One of the things that disturbed me most, early in my disability, was that when I lost my visibility, I was no longer called upon for help or ideas. I know people assumed I had enough to deal with, but I should have been the sole judge of it.

Safety is another factor, which we must consider. When you are weakened by disability, your vulnerability as a woman is magnified. At home I have my pistol to rely on, but the outside world is another matter. Having someone offer to accompany or transport you to a meeting or social event is a tremendous relief.

Don't be afraid to ask what caused the health problems. Through information we can make it easier for someone else. It's understood that most people aren't aware of the situations that exist unless they personally know someone whose life injury or illness has touched. I believe that disability is like race: unless you live it on a day to day basis, you can't possibly understand how all encompassing it really is.

By understanding, promoting and planning ways that will allow us to become more visible, you will insure that a valuable segment of society is not forgotten.

For today, the MS is in remission. I use a cane when I go out. It prevents falls when vertigo or weakness suddenly strike. Once a month I receive "trigger" injections of cortisone, lidocaine and Novocain in my neck and back to help control some of the pain from severe muscle spasms. I also take a drug that helps with seizures, anxiety, and muscle tremors that had been keeping me from sleeping. It has side effects like many drugs, but I'll trade them for a decent night's sleep.

HELP, I'VE FALLEN, AND NO ONE HAS EVEN NOTICED

When I was diagnosed with multiple sclerosis in 1979, my neurologist said to avoid stress. I didn't take his advice seriously. Stress was one of those middle class words that lost something in its translation to real life. Throughout my story you will see an over abundance of stress. At this late date, it occurs to me that avoiding stress wasn't the problem. Understanding, managing and confronting it in ways that related to my lifestyle were the answers I needed.

Before I started writing this article I discussed our family history with my mother. I needed her opinion to clarify my memory on many of our childhood ailments and customs. I specifically wanted to know about many of the superstitions. She informed me that she didn't know of any superstitions.

I asked, "What about when you were a baby and whooping cough was going around? You told us your parents took you to a neighbor who had a black stallion and had it blow its breath in your face. Because of that belief, you were protected." "That wasn't a superstition," she replied. "It worked."

Another treatment that worked: when one of us would step on a nail and puncture our foot, Mom would grease the nail and put it over the front door frame. If any evil spirits came in they would slide back out, and we wouldn't get an infection.

Her kind looks turned to puzzlement as I continued asking questions. It was the kind of look you give a census taker or social worker who knows nothing but what they learn in some school of higher learning. I became the dreaded stranger who brought fear and disgrace through the front door. By saying out loud what our life was like, and calling it superstitious, I shamed her. If I had been as kind and wise as she always was I would have phrased my questions differently.

The environment wasn't an easy subject to discuss either. Since we didn't live in a house that had running water until after I was fourteen years old, I wanted to talk about our water supply. Mom said our drinking water couldn't have been polluted because it always looked clean. The only "polluted" water Mom remembered hearing about was a dead rat that was found in the town reservoir. Many things in our life were, and always will be, a simple matter of faith.

Our water came out of a wooden trough, embedded in a hillside. It was strip mined for coal years earlier. The abandoned mineshaft near it was one of our favorite places to play. Runoff from the mines around our small town turned the river reddish yellow and killed the fish and other living things. Who knew what poisons these mines exuded or what they would do to humans? (Years later the mine owners were forced by law to plant trees and treat the water). Humans were and are another matter. I hear frequent stories of cancer and multiple sclerosis, etc. This was the background we emerged from. Myths, superstitions, "old wives' tales," lack of education and poverty coated us like a cocoon and protected us from nothing.

There were eighteen children in my father's family. Some died at birth; others made it until childhood. Thirteen lived to adulthood. He was born in rural Georgia and was of Cherokee blood. He quit school in the third grade to help support his family. Dad was self educated, and was the smartest man I've ever known.

Mother was one of eleven children and one miscarriage. Her family lived in the mountains of Pennsylvania. She was Seminole and Irish. She finished the seventh grade and grieved forever her lost education.

We were raised in the area of my mother's birth. There were six live births and one miscarriage. I have three sisters and two brothers.

My earliest memories are of us living in a little three room shack that had no electricity or water. Mom washed our clothes out back in the creek. The creek was also our refrigerator. Raccoons and other animals would often steal the food we stored. The food would also spoil or become saturated with water. Although Mom canned food and other family members fished and hunted, there was never enough food. Hunger was a way of life you never get used to.

Winters were brutal. There was never enough clothes or bedcovers to keep us warm. Anything that would burn was placed in the wood stove; this included car tires. The smell was horrendous, and the stove would turn bright red from the heat. It's a wonder the house didn't catch fire.

At the age of two I was diagnosed as having a tapeworm. It's a worm made up of many segments and the sections keep breaking off. The head attaches itself to the stomach and it can grow many feet in length. It was thought that I got mine from eating raw meat.

Needless to say, my parents tried many home remedies. Anything suggested as a cure was given to me. I recall drinking quarts of sauerkraut juice. Another supposed cure was coconut milk. Since these items weren't part of our diet I can only assume they were thought of as exotic enough to work. They didn't.

Doctors suggested mixing kerosene and sugar on a tablespoon and having me eat it. Turpentine and sugar were also given. They told Mom if the tapeworm got hungry it would come up in my throat and choke me. In hindsight, I see that her cures were safer then those of the medical establishments. Let me add that when you hear someone sing, "A spoonful of sugar makes the medicine go down," don't believe it.

During these early years I had many asthma attacks. I was also prone to catching other illness and it always seemed to take me longer than others to recover.

At age ten I was hospitalized with what they thought was scarlet fever. I remember being acutely ill for two weeks, and I was placed in the isolation unit.

After the third week in the hospital, doctors requested permission from my parents to administer an experimental medicine in hopes of curing me of having a tapeworm. My parents were told if they gave their permission, no bill would be owed for my stay. Since these doctors were "educated," they had to know what was best. The thought of not having to pay this large hospital bill seemed like a miracle to them.

The medicine was so harsh that a rubber tube was inserted inside my nose and pushed down into my stomach. Even so, when the medicine was given, I started to vomit. I don't know what the medicine was, but it killed the tapeworm.

One evening in March of 1992, I was verifying several facts with my mother. I said, "You and Dad let them experiment on me, and for that the bill was paid?" Mother, who was then 73 years old and on oxygen 24 hours a day, replied, "Yes, wasn't that lucky?" Yes, in one respect it was really lucky. I had endured a horrible ordeal for years having that parasite inside of me. My parent's had just done things the way they were taught: don't question authority. It's enough that I know who the real culprits were, and I'll forever wonder why an experimental drug was given to a child still in recovery.

When generation after generation is caught in a web of poverty, alcoholism, numerous health problems and very little formal education, it becomes almost impossible to take control of your life. While there might be small pockets of change, the vast majority will not escape.

My parents worked extremely hard all of their lives. Dad was a carpenter. Mom cleaned other people's houses and did factory work. After graduation from high school in 1962, I joined my older sister and mother at the same textile factory.

The factory was hot in the summer and cold in the winter. Cotton dust was so thick you could barely catch your breath, and the noise from the sewing machines was deafening. I developed several allergies. I was eighteen at the time. Someone told my dad to take me to an ear, nose and throat doctor. The doctor suggested an ocean voyage. What were those home cures again?

As we grew older, health problems increased. (People with a First Nation background have the worst health statistics of any race.) Alcoholism, drug abuse, poverty, suicide, medical disease, you name it, if it's a hardship, there will be a high incidence of it being inherited. Among my mother, father, sisters, and brothers, we all have some form of arthritis. The men have alcohol problems. Most of us have asthma, emphysema, or chronic bronchitis. All have some form of skin disease, including vitiligo, psoriasis, or eczema. Diabetes, heart disease, gall bladder disease (two-thirds of First Nation people have gall bladder disease); endometriosis, high blood pressure, ulcers, and atherosclerosis effect most of the family. Hyperactivity is showing up more frequently. Cancer is prevalent. (My father died of lung cancer in 1990). I have multiple sclerosis and systemic lupus erythematosus. I'm also a cancer survivor. One of my brothers shows signs of developing multiple sclerosis.

All three of my sons have learning disabilities, as do many of our children and grandchildren. My oldest son has cardio-pulmonary sarcoidosis, diabetes and high blood pressure. He's had pneumonia numerous times. He survived MRSA in his brain. That was a near fatality. The middle son had hepatitis. (He got it fishing in polluted waters). He also had mononucleosis and continues to have numerous infections. He survived a heart attack. My neurologist says the likelihood of his developing MS is great. The youngest son has always had severe hay fever, food and bee sting allergies, vitiligo, and is a survivor of MRSA.

I am appalled as I write this. The thought of all three sons facing death in one year almost took me along with them. I've never wanted to outlive any of them. I thought this generation would be able to overcome past obstacles because the quality of our life has improved greatly. A full plate can feed the body, but it doesn't necessarily follow that it will repair past deficiencies. If anything, genetics seem to be multiplying the worsening of new and different illnesses. Jesus. What was assumed to be continuing bad luck is much more sinister.

* * *

During the thirteen years I was married, I gave birth to three children. With each pregnancy there was a noticeable decline in my health. My legs would go weak, and I would stumble and often fall. Doctors diagnosed this as just about everything.

In 1972, I gave birth for the last time. It was a difficult

pregnancy. I had a seizure in the eighth month. My obstetrician didn't want his patients to gain more than twenty pounds so he put me on Dexedrine, a diet pill. There were many days that I couldn't even force myself to eat. When the seizure occurred, a doctor at the local hospital took over my care.

Neurological symptoms kept occurring, but they would disappear before I could get an appointment with a doctor.

Throughout life I have been an avid reader. It has always been my means of escape. During the seventies, I started reading feminist articles and books. There was an instant feeling of kinship and understanding. I joined a feminist group and became involved in a number of issues. For the first time in my life, I was around non-relatives who respected and valued my opinion. It was a very heady time, and it gave me the courage to make some much needed changes. One of the changes was meeting Sue, and soon she and I with the children moved in together.

During March 1977, I was having severe pain in my side. Tests showed a large tumor where my left ovary should have been. The endometriosis was back. Surgery was done to remove the tumor and part of my right ovary where another growth had started.

The boys were confused and worried. They were eleven, seven and three years old. I was scared that I would die and their dad would regain custody. Sue and my family took turns babysitting the boys. Sue knew very little about children but learned fast.

After a few months of recovery, I started looking for employment. One of my brothers found me a job cleaning vacant houses for a real estate company. I turned it into a business and hired three other women to help.

In October of 1977, the pain in my right ovary became so painful that I was hospitalized. The surgeon wanted to save part of the ovary, but I insisted that all of it be removed. This piecemeal surgery was destroying me mentally and physically. I also refused estrogen therapy. There were dire warnings about being thrown into the "change of life" overnight. It occurred but I managed it with vitamins. Sue and I researched what vitamins would relieve the hot flashes, night sweats and mood swings. The regimen worked.

During the surgery, I later found out, the doctor had sutured my right ureter closed. When I kept complaining of the pain and that something was very wrong, the doctor released me and refused to see me again.

Two months later in December of 1977, I had major reconstructive surgery to remove four inches of my right ureter. It was then reimplanted in the bladder. A valve to prevent reflux into the kidney was also fashioned. It worked for a short while. Because the kidney was closed off for so long, a large nephrosis had occurred. I was told that two thirds of my kidney wasn't functioning, and the left kidney was swollen because of the overload.

After each surgery I would have bouts of pins and needles in my hands, stumbling, numbness and many other symptoms diagnosed as anemia or stress.

I was having urological problems that continued into 1978. I was hospitalized again in April because of blood in my urine. While there, I asked the doctor to look at a mole on my foot that looked suspicious.

A biopsy found that it was a malignant melanoma, and a section of my foot was removed. With this type of cancer you can have just one or five hundred. You can also pass the tendency to develop melanoma on to your children.

The numbness and pins and needles were more frequent now. It was decided that I should be given two transfusions of platelets, that I was anemic.

A new symptom kept happening: a burning pain in my spine. All x-rays were negative. My urologist was a great guy. He kept saying, "Judith, I know you are having all these symptoms, but I swear it's not a urological problem."

One afternoon in April of 1979, I was overwhelmingly tired so I took a nap. During the sleep, I dreamed a wild bird was in the house. We were trying to get it outside without hurting it. (A wild bird in the house is a very bad omen). I woke up terrified.

When I tried to stand up I discovered my left side was

paralyzed from my eye on down. Sue took me to the emergency room. They gave me the name of a neurologist to call for an appointment.

On my first appointment, a basic neurological exam was conducted. The doctor tested my sense of touch, smell and hearing. I followed an object's movement with my eyes and walked a straight line to see if gait variations were evident. Many things were tried to elicit the correct response from the brain.

I then had an EEG. While I was trying to get the paste out of my long hair, the doctor went out to speak with Sue in private. He told her he thought the melanoma had spread to my brain, and the chances of survival were slim. She was also told not to tell me.

Naturally, she told me right away. We were devastated. Every other time there had been hope, but this time called for the planning of an ending not a recovery. I made out a will and a medical power of attorney that gave Sue medical decision making powers.

When a CAT scan of the brain showed no evidence of a tumor, the diagnosis was changed to a stroke.

A month later I had another episode of paralysis. My vision and speech were also affected. A physical therapist made me promise I wouldn't let anyone try to tell me it was all in my head. She knew that women were often suspected of having over active imaginations.

I made a decision to change doctors. I was hospitalized, and the testing began again. A lumbar puncture was done. It was the sickest week of my life. I couldn't get out of bed. Every time I sat up I started to vomit. It took a week for the needle stick to heal. This test and other observations gave a firm diagnosis. I had multiple sclerosis: the great crippler of young adults. (Diagnosis has now been made easier with MRI, Magnetic Resonance Imaging).

In 1981, I had the worst MS exacerbation to date. I was in the hospital for five and a half weeks. No part of my body seemed exempt from damage. During this time, I developed many opportunistic infections that weakened me further. I was unable to walk, and spasticity developed in both arms and legs. They brought me home in a wheelchair, and it looked like I would remain in one. I required home nursing care. This was what I thought all people with MS could expect. I wish someone had told me that every case was different, and that many people with MS never needed a wheelchair. It would have lessened the worry considerably.

Throughout this time everyone kept telling me to reduce the stress in my life. Testimonials will verify that my idea of stress prevention is in itself stressful. I am not a quiet person. I am not a calm person. Isn't that what stress reduction means?

Over and over during this ordeal everyone, including doctors, would say, "You don't look sick, you look good." It has become a long-standing joke among us that whenever a new health crisis occurs, we say, "But you look good." A compliment instead of a cure doesn't seem like an equal trade, but hey, that's just my opinion.

It has been twenty-two years since I was diagnosed with multiple sclerosis. The doctor responsible for the diagnosis continued to treat me even though I was on SSI and medical assistance. When he became interested in research he assumed that I would be a willing subject. Someone who once was a caring person turned into one of the most callous people I have ever known. In 1999 I found another neurologist. I view him with cautious eyes that cut deeper than a scalpel.

My neurologist has been trying trigger injections and stretching and spraying to alleviate the horrible headaches I get from muscle spasms. The injections consist of three drugs. I believe they are Lidocaine, Novocain and cortisone. They are injected directly into the muscle spasms along my shoulder blades, neck and sometimes the base of my skull. It is very painful, and unfortunately it is not a permanent cure. However, it does bring relief, and sometimes that is blessing enough.

In 1990, I started taking Amitriptyline. It's a mood elevator that helps with sleep at night and lessens the intensity of up and down emotions. I realized that I couldn't handle that side of MS any longer. It was unfair to everyone around me that I couldn't deal with treating it. My reluctance was due to wanting not to appear weak. I have no problem contemplating suicide, but admitting the need for a drug to control my emotions is embarrassing.

One of the most aggravating health problems I have is a skin disorder. It has been diagnosed as just about everything. The last diagnosis was eczema. Sue said that was a word that could mean just about anything. We assume it's just another sign of my immune systems failure.

I thought when I started this article that I could contribute some insight into dealing with an incurable illness. However, I have gained more than I have given. Putting everything down in black and white has given me the answers to questions I have been asking for years.

* * *

Bottom line, whatever is affecting you needs a label. I could function once my enemy was revealed. With MS, all of your systems can be impacted, and symptoms can come and go in rapid succession. It leaves you open to a diagnosis of hypochondria or mental instability. Hell, you even doubt yourself. My father-in-law had MS and was in a wheelchair the last fifteen years of his life. He was also confined to a veteran's hospital during these years. He died seven years before I was diagnosed.

We all say, "I know just how you feel," when discussing someone's illness. No, you don't. You can empathize, but that's as close as you'll get. I often wish I could have been more understanding with Mr. Witherow, but we have this tendency to feel it would be imposing to ask personal questions. I know from experience that I have gained the bulk of my knowledge about MS, as well as other diseases, from talking to people who were battling the same problem. Also, reading everything I could find and staying up to date on research helped greatly. Don't believe that your doctor has the time to stay up to date on everything.

Knowing someone with MS can have its drawbacks. I thought I would manifest everything my father-in-law did. Nothing was further from the truth. Everyone is different and you may or may not exhibit the symptoms you see others get.

To date, no doctor has really discussed with me what to expect from multiple sclerosis. Do doctors think we will manifest the symptoms if they discuss them with us? It seems to me that lack of information is the problem. When we are allowed to be partners in our healthcare, the trust benefits both parties, and the fear of the unknown can be dispelled.

Over the years I have become friends with three other women who have MS. We compare notes and cross check what is happening to our health. We all have different degrees of disability. Two of the women have gone blind for weeks at a time, and then their sight returned. I recently developed optic neuritis and have lost some of my vision. I have been using high doses of steroids since March 1994.

We understand intimately the problem of mood swings. The high highs are as disconcerting as the low lows. Mood elevators are prescribed often. Your mental and physical health are of equal importance. I no longer take Amitriptyline because of problems with my heart. I now take a drug called Klonopin. It works for seizures, insomnia, mood swings, and it keeps my legs from jerking so violently at night that they wear holes in my sheets.

In December of 1992, I almost died of cardiac arrest. There are two extra electrical pathways in my heart. One was ablated after two tries in January and April of 1993. Ablation is an electrophysiology specialty of some cardiologists. They burn the errant pathways out with radio frequency. It's my extreme bad luck that a second pathway is also there. One end of it was stunned on January 29, 1994. Within a day the tachycardia was back. I am now on Tambocor to keep my heart beating normally until another ablation can be done on June 8, 1994. The cardiologist said, "I will have to wait until then because you are at maximum radiation level." I asked him how the radiation would get out and he replied, "Oh, it just dissipates." I then asked him if breast cancer would be a problem, and he nonchalantly said, "I think you should be more concerned about leukemia or lymphoma." Since then, I have found out that these procedures are not even FDA approved. No one told me anything except that with the extra pathways, I risked death. Since that had almost happened, I thought I had no other choice. I now know there are other less dangerous options, but it is a bit late for me not to see this out to the end.

Guilt, anger, fear, sadness, etc., are natural parts of any illness. You are entitled to these feelings. With MS your moods can alter radically because this is part of the disease itself.

I've gone through times when I couldn't put names in alphabetical order. It makes using address and phone books a challenge. Other times I'm not able to make change. I have difficulty doing anything in sequence. Others mention the same problems. I'm experiencing short term memory bouts now. I just say every day is Saturday, and I am constantly amazed at what the date is. I can only assume the bill collectors are experiencing the same thing.

You are told repeatedly not to get over tired because it will make the muscle weakness worse. Excessive heat also weakens. While both are true, you do things when the energy is there in case it doesn't last. It's a judgment call.

What I've missed most is not being able to make long term plans. The changing nature of MS and even excitement over an upcoming event can exacerbate symptoms. I've learned not to mention plans until I'm sure I can carry them out. This way no one feels let down.

Possibly one of the hardest things to deal with is loss of bowel or bladder control. There are various medicines to lessen the problem, but the results do not seem that effective. One of my friends has the bowel problem, and it has been a nightmare for her. I have bouts with loss of bladder control, and when this happens, I take Urecholine.

The first time I had a really bad attack of vertigo, I thought it must be an earthquake. What I couldn't figure out was why only I seemed to notice. Over the counter drugs such as Bonine or Dramamine work as good as anything doctors prescribe.

A good sense of humor can be a blessing. It can put others at ease when they are feeling your pain, and it can help you maintain your sanity when the crazy nature of this disease gets to be too much.

Humor is fine, buy nothing compares to the love of a partner who instills the desire to live because we are one.

* * *

Learn that medical equipment can make life easier. It's not an admission of disability; it's just common sense. I use a cane (a flashy engraved green one), and I'll use whatever it takes to keep me as mobile as possible. Broken bones can cause an exacerbation of MS so preventing falls is very important.

Infections of any kind should be treated promptly. Use a dishwasher to sterilize all eating utensils whenever possible. Try to keep others away when they have colds, flu, etc. Watch out for opportunistic germs if hospitalized. It's no coincidence you pick up secondary infections during your stay. With your immune system weakened, you are at greater risk.

Have someone reorganize your living space. Put things at wheelchair height if needed so they can be reached without having to use a stool that is unsteady. Use smaller containers for milk, etc. When muscles are weakened, everything becomes twice as hard to lift.

Your sense of hot and cold may become diminished. Be careful of bath water and heating pads.

If you have trouble holding a pen, pencil or eating utensil, place foam rubber around them. The added size will help your grip; they are particularly beneficial if you have arthritis.

* * *

My greatest fear is for the future: not mine but that of my sons, grandchildren, and that of my families. Scientists now believe there may be a familial link to MS. I would like to know if I passed this on to any of my sons. They have a mother and grandfather with MS. Also, one son married a young woman whose grandmother had it. What does this do to increase the risk in their two children?

Recently I was told that four members of one family from my

hometown have MS. This was one of the families my mother worked for. There is also a man whose family I worked for with the same diagnosis. It is well known that multiple sclerosis isn't contagious so what is the common denominator here? In a town of approximately 450 people, it is more than a coincidence that so many have MS. These are the hard questions that still need answers.

Knowing ahead of time that you could acquire a particular disease might not alter the course of it, but it could ease the nightmare of trying to get a firm diagnosis sooner.

I need to believe that with all of the research being done on AIDS, a cure for other immune system disorders, including MS, will be found.

There is now the overwhelming realization of what my family is facing. Not quick certain death but a slow torturous one that will be endured for time without end.

I cannot repair the ongoing damage to the earth. Nor will I try to replace family superstition with the harsh words of truth. I will watch and wait like the government does and pretend nothing is wrong. But unlike the government, I will assist and ease the suffering whenever possible. When the time is right, I will pass this knowledge on to another. I will whisper that it is not evil spirits or bad luck. It is much much scarier than that.

GROUP THERAPY FOR THE UNINITIATED

Night, without fail, unseals my eyelids like some half-licked envelope flap. Does it still believe it will catch me napping and carry me painfully away?

How can I gain the strength to attend our support group this morning? Everything hurts but my earlobes and several broken strands of hair. No. Staying home isn't an acceptable option. I need to go. These women share my same bed of illnesses. Many of them will look and feel worse than I do.

Sue, does it seem like I'm giving away clothing faster than a dead relative's family? Please help me look for clothing to wear that fits. Reed thin women are considered more desirable in this country, but try losing weight the muscle wasting way. Don't tell me I look good! Good stopped after sixty pounds of quick weight loss. Your eyes still see the young woman you met twenty-five years ago.

I hear the same weight statement from other women, but many of them are at the opposite end of the weight scale. Steroids to help control some of the symptoms can cause varying amounts of weight gain. They also cause calcium loss in the bones. Osteoporosis gets added to our list of diseases caused by medications that supposedly slow damage.

At group I know that a chalkboard will be waiting. It will be filled with words to help us cope with our disease. They hold the answer to things some of us intimately know but if a new person arrives we'll discuss them once again.

These "step" words are used at various groups. Our particular group is one with a five-step program. The words are **Anger, Bargaining, Depression, Denial** and **Acceptance**. We have been taught that you don't stay at any one step. You move back and forth using the word that best describes where you are at the moment.

Bargaining. It's called **Bargaining**. It's one of the words I hear the facilitator repeat. You strike a bargain with whomever it is you believe in. This is where you weave between praying and promising--sweating and swearing. I don't know what I did to deserve this, but I'll try to make amends. Why does trouble always find my change of address card? The philosophical side of me asks, If not me, who? Who deserves this much ill health?

The Spirits dare me to name names. Sorry, but that's a line of spaces I choose to leave blank. Things can always get better, but here sits a woman who has watched them go in the opposite direction numerous times. Allow someone who hasn't been properly humbled to answer that question. Call on another woman who has less immune system diseases than I do.

I will speak aloud the name of one of my diseases. Systemic lupus. It has brought me to this particular group. Like many other women of color I was chosen by lupus. It pulls in new recruits faster than your connective tissue can fray. It's another disease that has very little money for research despite the fact that it out numbers other well-known incurable illnesses by a wide margin. Whenever "it strikes women more often" is heard, the battle for funding automatically begins. When you add the predominance of women of color you have two strikes, and you're about to take the third swing that signals—"You're Out!"

"She Who Does Not Have Lupus" tells us our goal is to work towards **Acceptance**. "Do not give up and do not give in, but try to accept the diagnosis of your disease." Maybe it was phrased differently, but I was busy rearranging my swollen hip joints. A padded chair would certainly feel good, wouldn't it? I'll write myself a reminder to bring a cushion next time. It's a scrap of information that comforts me more than the words I'm trying to concentrate on.

SHE continues doing the job she has been trained to do. **Anger**. "It's perfectly normal that you feel angry. Only someone in **Denial** would feel otherwise." SHE is very good at what she does. That is not enough. The knowledge I crave can only come from the other "chosen" ones.

Wouldn't it be more helpful if I shared my theory of how lupus entered my body? How years of drinking run-off water from coal mines did more than quench my thirst. If crying could drain my body of toxins via my tear ducts, perhaps I'd try. But where would you store so much poison until a safe means of disposal could be found? My secrets have to be whispered to the wind until the time is right. The words will endlessly echo the reason why I think there's so many immune system diseases among family, friends and others.

Until something better comes along I will listen as SHE explains the steps we need to survive until a cure is found. The steps may help some but today they only serve to heighten my **Depression**.

I contemplate whether today will be one of the last times I walk the seemingly endless distance to the meeting room. The rheumatologist has advised me to start using a wheelchair before I fracture a hip. That would not only be depressing—it could be life threatening. After previously breaking numerous bones the thought of hip or knee surgery causes a mental fall down all five of the steps. (Lupus destroys cartilage and puts your joints at greater risk).

Thinking about the loss of walking causes me to envision starting another Step Program. It would contain the letters-- R.A.M.P.—Rage Against Major Planning. It would teach others about the difficulty life's barriers entail. Going through regular sized doorways, shopping in stores where the aisles are cluttered with merchandise, trying to reach something while seated in your wheelchair, finding a handicapped parking place, educating doctors about effective pain medicine, etc., etc., etc. This is beyond depressing.

Until all women's health becomes a priority, many will die or become disabled, without even knowing the name of what crippled or murdered them. It's not enough to give a donation, make a phone call or send a get well card. Disability is a 24/7 way of life. Spend enough time with someone so you know what a "day in the life" is really like. It won't give you the entire truth, but it will be a big step towards understanding. You can walk away and go about your life, but my bed of illnesses is a forever deal. Does that sound like **Anger**? No. It's the inescapable truth.

CAN YOU FEEL THE PAIN?

November 28th, 2003 I read an email, a letter and answered a phone call from friends who are living the life of incurable illnesses along with me. These contacts were from women friends who used to be in our lupus support group. It was back when we were able to attend meetings on a monthly basis and support each other in person. Over the past five years we have all stopped attending group at varying rates. Reading the email made me feel worse than I did when I woke up this morning. Waking up four times during the night didn't make thinking about the worsening health of others easier.

It occurred to me that I haven't read anything about what happens when the one who also needs answers and support, becomes a caregiver to others who turn to you for help. When I take the time to think about it—which I try not to do—it becomes more than a bit overwhelming. It didn't take long for the weariness to turn into righteous, rightful anger. Where in the hell are the supposed medical practitioners who shamelessly hold out their hands to collect money for writing a few 'scripts, (prescriptions) and remind you to make your next depressing appointment? Depressing, and near useless, but "What if" will find you dragging your body back for another go 'round.

I don't need them to recite hypocritically that it's a shame that I have an incurable disease. A shame? It was way past a frigging shame fifteen years ago. I have more than one incurable illness, but the main shame I feel is towards a country that spends more on war than it does on research for saving lives.

The other shame that I'm forced to swallow is finding myself trying to comfort sisters with words concerning what treatments are available. There is always the hope that one of us will hear something that might help in even the slightest way. Some things work for a short period, but other times have worsened symptoms for me. However, I hear myself parroting words about treatments that have bought me a little more time, and hopefully a little less pain. (Judith there is no cure for lupus!) Some days the entire situation makes me question why I fight so hard to live. There are times I've prayed for death to take me to the other side. I'm writing these words, but my heart would finish breaking if I were to say them out loud and cause someone to lose hope.

When someone holds onto the hope you know something that will help relieve some of her symptoms, or have learned a way to manage pain more effectively, you better put yourself in the pulpit and do more than pass the collection plate for yourself.

Perhaps I should mention AGAIN that lupus is an autoimmune disease that affects women, mostly women of color, 90-some percent of the time. I've lived with it for more than a decade, and the livin' certainly hasn't been easy. Don't blow me off as a whiner. Although, I could justifiably be one, I don't have the concentration or interest to waste on something else that's as useful as a rope on a goat.

For numerous years I haven't been treated with any new medicines prescribed for systemic lupus or multiple sclerosis. The same mind and body breaking treatments are still being used as they were when I was first diagnosed. I'm on my third form of immune suppressant. To say that I have much of a workable immune system is something I write to comfort myself. I want to believe that at least some medicines are working to suppress the mutant cells in my body. When reality sinks in, I remind myself that whenever I'm around others there is the risk of catching something that could be fatal.

Truth Time: Can anyone conceive of constantly being on guard when you're with your partner of numerous years? Does the thought of her touch, the one that always brought such joy, being replaced by caution and fear allow you to understand the magnitude of what is happening? How would you maintain a safe, loving relationship? A relationship where you don't have to give serious thought to every aspect of the act of lovemaking. It's beyond AIDS and other illnesses. We're talking the simple act of kissing or the exchange of saliva. If you can't get helpful medical advice from your doctor, what type of safe sex advice do you think a lesbian will receive?

Tell me that you honestly feel the depth of this medical madness and the mental pain it inflicts? I sincerely hope that the majority of you were only able to imagine it in the terms of my definition.

Excuse me if I'm rambling, but I'll get back to the main focus of this article shortly. Words and structure are taking longer these days. This is pure "H" hell for a writer.

Last night I was trying to organize numerous pieces of medical receipts and lab reports. At one point I found a packet of pictures of discoid skin lesion eruptions that Sue had taken during several years of flares. They covered large areas of my body. We were both shocked at how horrible they appeared. I spoke frankly about the unbearable pain they had caused. We looked at the dates written on the back of the photos. Many were taken before I was diagnosed with systemic lupus.

During this period of time I was constantly reading about neurological and autoimmune diseases. I had a sinking feeling that something unrelated to multiple sclerosis was taking place. A number of the symptoms I was encountering weren't ones associated with MS. I began to underline symptoms pertaining to lupus in our Merck Manual. It is an invaluable medical resource book.

During the next outbreak of lesions I allowed them to get completely out of control then made an appointment with a dermatologist. I insisted he do punch biopsies of the lesions in hope of finally receiving a correct diagnosis. This needed to be done before any treatment could be started.

He told me that I would have to pay for the tests because my insurance wouldn't pay for anything that a doctor hadn't ordered. Let's just say that I scared him enough that he wanted to do the tests and get me out of his office. Pain and ignorance that cause me further harm do not allow me to be polite or have myself pushed beyond further endurance.

To make years of a seriously long story shorter, the tests came back acutely positive for lupus. The ANA amount was off the wall for positive lupus. My primary care doctor's response at my next visit—"Judith, you already have one incurable disease. I didn't want to tell you that you have another." In all calmness, on the outside, I'll say, "NOT WANTING ME TO HAVE ANOTHER ILLNESS DIDN'T PREVENT IT!" He wasted years of treatment that only the Spirits know if it would have made a difference in my health today. Please, get away from anyone who treats you in this life-shortening manner.

DIRECT QUOTES FROM SISTERS WITH LUPUS:

Email—"Judith, My health has been bad (frowning face symbol) Firstly, I have been having seizures and as a result my prednisone (steroid) has gone up. I'm fat as hell! To top it off I'm on Cytoxan. I need six treatments and I have had three already. I sit there for four or five hours while they give it to me intravenously. They call it chemotherapy. My hair is still intact, but I get sick in the stomach a lot and I have the shakes. How are you doing? I'm wearing a wig but because my face is so round the elastic is all stretched out. Love,--"

Letter—"Judith, The new pain dosage seems to be better but it hurts like hell to take the patch off. My husband uses baby oil, soap and Vaseline to try to get it off. I start crying before he even removes the patch—now I know why they call them PAIN PATCH. I take hydrocodone for the breakthrough pain and I still can't sleep at night so I take Xanax and some time if I'm not up every two hours going to the bathroom then I can sleep. I take Carbatrol for seizures. My face is as big as an apple pie (smile) and I have worn down every pair of shoes in my closet. I have started giving piano lessons to help my income and I have three students. See you—"

Phone Call: "Judith-Thank you so much for the birthday card. I had to laugh at the picture of the high heels on the front and the ugly flat shoes on the inside." (We both laughed.) "I show the card to everyone. It is so true. I went from very high, to high, now as low as I can get, but my feet kill me." Judith, I'm not doing well at all. How are you doing? I have five different sizes of clothes that I switch back and forth wearing. Those damned steroids! (How much do you take?) I'm taking 60mgs. again. I just feel so bad all of the time. Everyone wants to talk about the holidays coming up and I just want to pull the covers over my head. Crying sounds. Listen, Honey, I love you but I'll have to talk to you later. Goodbye and love to Sue also."

Isn't it ironic that because of the way society views women that everyone put the main emphasis of their disease on weight gain? Even to the point of not taking certain medicines because of what others might say or think. I could logically discuss all of the crap concerning weight gain, but what could I write that isn't already known about self-concept?

Despite the hellish nature of the correspondence I was able to supply some help for some of the problems. I told my sisters that I had discovered a way to remove adhesive with out breaking our thin skin caused by lupus. It can also be used to remove adhesive from a colostomy connection, nicotine patches and especially for anyone who needs to use pain patches on a regular basis. The name of the product is: Uni-Solve Adhesive Remover Wipe. It can be bought at medical supply stores or you can have your pharmacy order it. This product is for anyone who is sensitive to adhesives for whatever reason. I still can't believe what a difference it has made when Sue changes my pain patch every 72hrs. The name of the pain patch I use is Duragesic. It comes in doses from 25mgs. to 100mgs and it works by slowly being released into the body in regular amounts. (The medicine in it is Fentanyl.)

Steroids and immune suppressants—Cytoxan, Metholtrexate and Immuran cause numerous problems with thrush throughout the body. Nyastatin Cream USP, 100.000 units per gram works well for thrush under your breasts, etc. Diflucan is used for vaginal yeast infection as well as numerous other areas of the body. Nystatin Oral Suspension works well for thrush inside the mouth and digestive system. Thrush is a major problem when your immune system is compromised. Thrush inside your mouth and gut can keep you from eating the foods that is necessary to keep your strength up. Thrush usually thrives in warm, moist areas. It's important to deal with these problems immediately. They may seem trivial compared to other symptoms, but I'm not on a first name basis with all of them because I like the taste or feel of any of them.

Another medicine that has helped me repeatedly is Zovirax Ointment 5% (acyclovir). It's used especially when your immune system is compromised to treat herpes simplex—cold sores. They appear repeatedly because of lowered immune system, stress, and infection from others. I have discovered that eating peanuts or garbanzo beans will cause a blister to develop on my lip within hours of eating either food. Again, I don't know the correlation, but an outbreak occurs every time I have accidentally ingested anything from these food groups. Another thing worthy of mention is that alfalfa sprouts should be avoided if you are immune suppressed.

Being able to help in a small or large way in lessening pain or symptoms is enough to put my own life in perspective. Today I can type and believe that it's enough to keep me going because it makes a difference in quality of life. My one friend no longer cries at the thought of having her pain patch changed. It is a real upper for me when I hear this statement. However, it doesn't lessen my belief that the medical establishment needs to find out the same answers that I stumble across. Knowing what I do I won't trust any bit of information to chance. Instead, I make it a point to enlighten every doctor and medical association with what I know about this one product in particular. After asking two doctors about Uni-solve, and both of them being clueless concerning the adhesive remover, I believed that further research didn't need to be wasted while others suffered.

I owe this article to my group therapy sisters. They are the ones who constantly try to get me to try a hair weave. I don't think so! And, it's not because my hair is about two inches long. (One of the most recent symptoms I have developed is called "Lupus hair." It means that my hair is breaking off instead of falling out at the roots.)

Nor will I go with them to get fake nails even if they pay. If they'll go with me for my fourth tattoo—a rainbow cuff around my left wrist—I'll discuss their femme ideas. I'll also help them shop for the combat boots they've always teased me about. Peace and health for all of us in 2005.

GRAINS OF PAIN

Mother Fate you almost had me.
You left an active mind in a
body that keeps ignoring all
physical commands messing
up my hour-glass of time.
Instead of trickling
smoothly onward
it's hung up
in the
middle.
Each grain that
now struggles through
does so with great effort,
a cruel hoax to mimic movement.
I've learned not to confuse desire
with progress, thereby freeing myself to
dream my dreams. In this I'm unrestricted.

NIGHT NOT YET FALLEN

Sleep, my former protectress,
why have you deserted me?

How could one who repaired
each new day's devastation
slow the cradle that lulled me?
Leave not these eyes awake
each night in an atmosphere
inhabited by torturous demons.
Chill not my being with
thoughts of those who
wedged the door ajar.
Squeeze tightly these
unrelenting eyelids with
hands of tempered steel.

Make me sightless to all
but my dreamland oasis.

FEMINISM

- Equality

- Political

- Progressive

Advocating social, political,
legal, and economic
justice for all.

FEMINISM—THREE SCORE AND FOUR

From birth it can be assumed that I was my own woman. Feminist wasn't a word yet conceived. Throughout my younger years the phrase, "She is so different," was overheard by me. Overheard but discarded as was the word, Tomboy.

My father was the only one who seemed to understand me completely. He was Cherokee, and recognized that I was truly two spirited. He taught me to box, and he railed out constantly to have my sister's do the "female" work. It was accepted that I would go fishing, hunting, play sports or do whatever my culture involved. From the age of twelve I owned a .12 gauge shotgun—still do. I refuse to allow others to define what I should or shouldn't ascribe to when it comes to my race. With that laid to rest I'll continue writing about women and their rights.

In 1962 I wrote a report in English class about the Suffragette Movement in Great Britain. I can't remember where the information was found, but I knew that it appealed to me greatly. It gave credence to my belief concerning the inequality between the sexes. At the time my teacher seemed as mystified as the majority of the world concerning why I chose that particular subject to write about.

As was the custom I married because it was expected. During this ten year period I played on a women's softball team. I fought to become the first female umpire on the Little League team in our county and won. I was booed every time I took the field. It would have been considered unethical if this was done to a man, but no one was going to stop me from doing what I considered fair. During this time girls were joining the teams. Seeing the treatment they were also receiving I quit umpiring after talking another woman into taking my place.

I became an assistant manager and put a fifth grade girl in the starting position of pitcher. Another round of name calling and anger ensued. She was shy and didn't want to stand up to the adults, and the boys who believed in their right of male privilege and position. If she hadn't been the best player for this position I wouldn't have asked her to endure the idiocy of others. I promised that if she would pitch in one game and it turned out to be a mistake the subject would never come up again. Every pitch she threw whizzed past the batter in the strike zone. With each throw the crowd became quieter and quieter. It was hard to not to toss back the war whoops that I'd been putting up with for two years.

This is how we teach young girls to believe in equality. It doesn't always come naturally in society. If all of us learned the fine art of mentoring—hard though it might be the change we've been craving could be achieved.

In the early seventies I became active in the women's movement. It was the first time there was a place that welcomed my voice and expertise in any number of areas. One of my first jobs was putting out a newsletter for our chapter in N.O.W. Through working on different events I became a writer who could explain to others what was taking place in various feminist activities. I've remained a writer throughout the decades, and have added photography to document the changes and events that have occurred.

Many women have left the movement for one reason or another. It's an ongoing problem to encourage young women to join and fight for the rights they believe have already been gained. We've changed numerous laws, and ways of thinking, but there is still a long way to go. Until we can get a woman elected president without the media refusing to give equal coverage and respect we haven't achieved the goals we've worked on for countless decades.

Until we can regain the feminist bookstores, shops, networks, etc. we have not achieved the goals that were laid out with the belief that what we were fighting for would surely be recognized by both sexes without question.

Unless we can get through a year without hearing about one or more of our publications facing demise, because of lack of subscribers or donations we haven't succeeded. It's beyond pathetic that we can't rise up and make sure the women who are doing the day to day work has the funds to be allowed to keep us informed. Instead, part of their valuable time needs to be used begging for the right to work their asses off without pay!

Numerous times I've been asked how much I get paid for the articles I write for different feminist sources. Stop laughing! No amount of money could pay for the bookcase piled high with copies I've received in lieu of payment. Many don't understand my way of thinking, but I'm not going to quit until we either succeed or I've passed over to another place. Hopefully, it will already have everything that I've worked tirelessly for in this world.

DON'T BLAME ME, I VOTED FOR MYSELF

On November 5, 1996 I did not vote for Bill C., Ross P., Bob D. or any other Guy running for the office of president. Nor did I cast my ballot for the various secondary parties at the bottom of the wannabe list. These parties were also led by Guys trying to separate me from my conscience via the voting booth.

This election year I needed to do something I could live with. For over twenty years I have written about and participated in numerous pickets, protests and causes. The possibility of change has always burned brightly within me, but this presidential election decidedly changed all of that. When I kept hearing feminist friends as well as national feminist leaders that I trust say "We have to vote for the lesser of two evils," I knew my bottom line and my gag threshold were on a collision course. Perhaps others could devalue their vote, but mine was not going to be used to further the agenda of someone whose own party affiliation couldn't be determined. Here stood a woman who was too broke to buy that concept.

I had always voted the Democratic ticket in the past, but this time I couldn't find a presidential candidate who resembled a Democrat in ideology. Since childhood my impoverished family indoctrinated me with the belief that the Donkeys were for the people—and the poor—while the Elephants represented big business—and the rich. In 1996 I could find no preprinted name on the sample ballot worthy of the Donkey tag. Clinton lost his tag when he signed the so-called "welfare reform" bill and the Defense of Marriage Act.

As a thinking caring woman, the decision I had been agonizing over became clear. I would write in my own name. This became something that excited and interested me. There was no longer a need to vote for the lesser of any evil. Not that I was sainthood material, but there wasn't a tinge of evil around me either.

The criteria I used to judge others was applied to myself: Was I willing to make unpopular decisions that would benefit others, not just the chosen few and myself? Did I genuinely feel others' pain or was I just capable of squeezing out a tear for a photo opportunity? Would donations be used for the purpose intended? Would I rethink my position on friendship and understand that money could indeed buy me friends. So many friends that it might take other countries to hold them all? Did I inhale? If so, did I exhale? Would Sue, my partner of 20 years, make a presentable First Femme? Did I own a tuxedo? If not, was there a thrift store nearby? An unqualified Yes was given to each question asked.

I chose to run for president because I believed I was the best qualified among the candidates, and the past year has borne this out. We have seen our past social and economic accomplishments unravel at a pace that has not been equaled in decades. What used to be called entitlements to aid the least privileged of us are now venomous curses to incite those who have against those who never will have. Welfare, child care, Medicaid, affirmative action, subsidized housing, energy assistance, gays and lesbians in the military, SSI for those with alcohol or drug dependence, food stamps, government funded health clinics, domestic partnership, immigrant benefits, etc., etc.

Where were the Front-line Feminists who asked me to give it my all? I gave. I trusted, and I gave until it hurt. When the government cuts by the Elephant in Donkey Hide started affecting everyone around me, I couldn't buy the movement rhetoric that I'd been hearing for years. "Just wait, Judith, your time will come."

Well, it hasn't. You know that "glass ceiling" that everyone has been talking about? On looking up I find that after all I've done I don't have enough of it to install even the smallest of skylights. Why is my view of the sky still blocked by those who have climbed on their class privilege and sold out poor women so they could compete with the big Guys. Why can't they reach out to us, pulling us up until the swell from all the empowered women will crash the thickest of glass barriers?

A number of feminists were offended by my decision to throw my hat into the ring as a write-in presidential candidate. This surprised and saddened me. They told me I couldn't do it. I would answer, "Well, yeah, I can. I know how to spell 'Witherow.'" My answer appeared to be blasphemous to say the least. Negative reactions to my candidacy led me to believe that others didn't view me as their equal—much less their president. The horrific absurdity of what was going on in the real world seemed to be of little relevance. Couldn't these wise women see and feel the terror and helplessness in my decision? Did they honestly believe I could cause Clinton to lose? Excuse me, but if he was a loser, he was a loser on his own terms and lack of merit.

Clinton's first shot at four years of Democrat leadership still rings 'round the progressive world. "Don't Ask Don't Tell" sounds like a warmed over version of the Reagan's "Just Say No." Bill's support of DOMA finished negating his "Some of my best friends are" promises of the '92 campaign.

During the first term, signing the Welfare Deform Bill seemed of little significance while justifying corporate welfare was easy. Keep looking. It will become as plain as the Medicaid framed glasses on your face. You're about to be economically trickled on by yet another president.

While I agree with Hillary that it takes a village to raise a child, you better have a few elders around who sincerely care about its inhabitants. Elders who are not afraid to stick with their principles—much less the party that elected them--are needed. We don't need those who are in it for the short run. Nor the ones whose malnourished agenda have weakened us to the point of settling for the "Least of any evil."

Hillary was hung out to dry with her health care bill. She allowed herself to stay on that clothesline while Bill supplied the pins. So while Bill and Hillary's first term promises for universal access to health care were left blowing in the wind, Bill's second term budget cuts federal funding for health care. I live with systemic lupus, multiple sclerosis and other problems acquired from the diseases wallowing around in my gene pool. My body, poisoned by the environmentally destroyed strip-mined environs of my childhood, requires sixteen additional poisons daily—including chemotherapy and steroids—just to survive. I have fought and lost while my state tries to recover from diminished federal funding by turning over my health care to a for-profit HMO system. Now, instead of celebrating universal access to health care without a Medicaid label, I fear that my doctors will succumb to HMO incentives of more money for less treatment.

While we sweat the cuts Clinton laid on us in the newest budget balancing effort, military funding remains unscathed. My 48 year old sister, Josie, who works at a local gas station, supplied me with the statistics for the May 17 and 18th air show at Andrew's Air Force Base. (This is the home of the president's plane.) The event was billed as the Department of Defense Joint Services Open House. Half a million people were invited to ogle war toys and war games. Whenever I hear the words "open house" I know something is being sold. Just because something is being sold, do we really have to buy it? Josie said that customers were bitchin' 5 to 1 about the cost, necessity and congested roads in our area during this event. To fund this I receive less medical care?

True feminists and other progressives should have flocked to my been-there-don't need-a-crystal-ball outlook for the future rather than trying to shame me into voting for the lesser of the evils as they saw it. My way offered the least amount of harm and hurt to those already suffering from economic disparity.

Granted, my campaign started a bit late—October to be exact. And my energy level was probably not up to campaign standards because of my health. But, unlike other presidential candidates, I had no problem revealing my limitations. Did the medications affect my mental outlook? Not in any way that distorted the ugly truth—unfortunately.

My platform included a "tunnel to the future." I'd read and heard about way too many bridge collapses to buy into that other slogan. Not the light at the end of the tunnel either—that's a whole other concept. This campaign was to be totally woman identified. (If you have a psychoanalyst, ask her to explain it.) To questions that I couldn't or didn't want to answer, I replied, "I'm your president not your mother. Next question."

To complement my campaign, I asked for input from trusted experts. I tried not to quote famous people because they have a habit of changing their minds or crying "misquote." I relied on family and friends who would not mislead me. My sister Josie provided me statistics about the way things are from her perspective at the corner gas station. My son Mark alerted me to how the privileged live which he learns from servicing their air conditioning. My friend Michael from West Virginia offered me this tidbit: "the wealthiest 358 individuals in the world today possess as much combined wealth as the poorest two and a half billion people. The gap between rich and poor is now the greatest in our nation's history. In fact, there is a greater gap between rich and poor in the US than in almost any other industrialized country. More than one in five American children today lives in poverty."

And just what is the Democratic Party doing about it? And what are my feminist leaders who urged me to support the Democrats doing? I want more than "Feel Good Feminism." Don't give me any more speeches, books to buy, subscriptions to newspapers, appearances at parades where they are the ones down front carrying the banners. Give me something that shows you respect my opinion. If they have lost me, they are in more trouble than could ever be imagined. I've always been there. Been there, that is, until the last election.

The remaining question appears to be: do we allow our Font-line Feminists to continue to sell us out for a seat at the table? Or do we demand they practice the dogma they have always preached? No more spouting equality while practicing self-serving attitudes. Last but not least, no more "Least of all evils," slogans.

When you're driving down the road and you see a bumper sticker   that reads DON'T BLAME ME--I VOTED FOR GUY/GUY, remember that somewhere in Maryland there's a woman whose sticker reads DON'T BLAME ME--I VOTED FOR MYSELF.

YO' DONE BRIDGE IS FALLIN' DOWN

To quote Audre Lorde, "The Master's tools will never dismantle the master's house." With all due respect to Ms. Lorde, I wish she had continued on and said, "Nor use those tools to build on rooms and a glass ceiling for your self. Don't hone your skills with power tools and leave your sisters out of sight in the cellar."

Unfortunately, this is exactly what has happened. Some women have gotten a place at the proverbial table, while others are left to endure belly-touching-backbone hunger. I angrily watch as lawmakers shred entitlement programs. Where are my sisters? How long will they wait before organizing numerous others to join in this heartless fight?

Twenty-five years ago, when I joined the women's movement, I was constantly assured that after we worked on the ERA, abortion rights, pay equity, credit, sexual preference, etc., etc., we would put our energies into poverty. Countless times I was told, "Be patient, Judith." Patient? I've come to realize that patience is a word used to stifle dissent. It's also a word I hear when someone doesn't have a clear understanding of the magnitude of a problem. Welfare was another word that many others didn't want to hear. It was a four-letter word then. It is a capitalized four-letter word now. With the dismantling of entitlement programs, time has virtually run out. When are feminists going to take up the battle cry and come out in the same numbers as they did for every other cause?

Some are doing what they can—like the Welfare Warriors located in Milwaukee, Wisconsin. Their slogan is, "We are mothers in poverty working to make a difference for all of us." The key word is ALL. Coming from the poorest of the poor group—Native American--I understand this concept of a group or tribal effort.

It's hard to focus on any one issue of poverty. Through experience I've found that poverty has it greatest effect on health. Because of this belief I will try to explain what happens when culture, poverty, and racism collide on a personal level.

BELOW THE BOTTOM LINE

There was a time when I had a bottom line concerning my health. No experimentation. Never. Decades of watching how the medical community treated my family instilled this belief in me. Now, too much has happened to keep me from rooting around in their guinea pig pen. I'm willing to try treatments that have the barest chance of helping. Perhaps they will hurt, but what if they help? What I know for certain is that I live in this body alone. No one knows what my diseases feel like. Even the women who share this same bed of illnesses do not know.

Well meaning feminist friends believe they know what is best for me. Many times they get upset when I choose to make my own decisions and ignore their advice. This matronizing attitude leads me to believe that we are not so equal after all. If my decisions are not respected, then what is the definition of equality? Has twenty-five years of fighting for every woman's right to choose counted as naught? A lot of the time the answer is sadly, yes.

For many years I took the advice of those I thought were wiser. Wiser because they had degrees to prove their wisdom. My partner of twenty-two years has always told me that degrees prove privilege, not wisdom. I believe she can say this because she has a number of degrees and a job that people respect. If careers and education aren't important, why is it that they are the first two subjects discussed at many gatherings? Try entering these discussions with "high school" and "disabled." Heads will swivel faster than that girl's from the Exorcist.

The generations of female bodies who breathed life into me were silenced by my arrogance of assimilation. Perhaps with age I've gained the knowledge that no teacher, preacher or book could provide. It's of no comfort to realize that what I was seeking was among my own people. The ones who need the most help are all around me. That is where I can see the most progress or decline taking place first hand.

Coal mining companies and various factories polluted the land and water of my birthplace. Because of this environmental assault, my large family has many health problems. When you add generations of poverty, illiteracy, and abuse by the system, you don't need a crystal ball to determine your destiny. What you do need is a nation willing to provide health care to everyone regardless of his or her ability to pay.

Perceptions. You will have to accept mine as you would another's life work of research. If not, you will need to lay wide my brain with a scalpel and poke around inside until my truths become evident to you. Scoop out what useful fact or figure you need to support your theory or belief. What I know about illness, cures, and addictions comes from experience and firsthand stories. I believe myself to be intelligent enough to help others understand a way of life that might not be theirs. Sharing some of the information gained with someone else like myself is of even greater importance.

I've written a number of articles about my life of poverty and ongoing illness. But I'd rather get whipped with a keen switch than answer an oral question about my health. This same feeling of being invaded applies to giving out information about my family—majority Native American—and friends. For the purpose of this article, I will do both. (What I won't do is name specific tribes.) A combination of sadness, anger, and embarrassment fills me as I consider what details to discuss.

While I appreciate my friends and family's concern regarding experimental treatments, fear is not enough to still my longing to learn some truths. If I choose to enter an experimental program, I do it with as much knowledge as possible. Who should this research be done on? Less educated uninformed women who have no other option? Common sense tells me that the testing needs to be done on those who have the disease being researched. Don't I have the absolute right to choose to volunteer for testing? I need answers. I'm weary of being randomly served up like a tennis ball. My humanity cannot be bought, taught, or tested out of me. And yes, many times I am fooled. The will to live and be free from pain can cloud the senses and turn research into regret.

I strongly dislike seeing new medical people. The first thing they want is your medical history. That is to be expected. What isn't expected is my long list. It's like naming ex-lovers. Someone thinks she wants to hear the answer, but you'd better not have a very long list.

My list is very long—the medical one. Some of my diseases and surgeries: systemic lupus, multiple sclerosis, endometriosis, cancer, tapeworm, Bell's Palsy, fibromyalgia, vasculitis, osteoporosis, peripheral neuropathy, heart disease, kidney disease, gall bladder surgery, hysterectomy, left and right oophorectomy, appendectomy, osteoarthritis, etc., etc.

I take eighteen different medicines daily. Do they help? To quote my deceased father, "I'm not about to stop any of them to find out." Many of the illnesses listed cause considerable pain. Some days I spend curled up in a knot because it hurts too much to move. When this happens, the treatment I use is not prescribed or bought over the counter. Mother Earth supplies the relief to temporarily deny the demons. This down time is used to relive mentally how malnourished I was in childhood. I lay and fantasize about whether getting free lunch at school would have made a difference. The answer is always yes. It would have helped me concentrate on my schooling instead of the loudness of my belly's growling. I know that I would also be a healthier adult today if more emphasis had been placed on the feeding of my body. To begrudge any child food is an unspeakable evil. Many politicians have used this as a way to save money. Little or no fight was put up when it happened in the early eighties.

Whenever some politician or newscaster talks about "those people" on SSI, welfare, or Medicaid, it intensifies the pain. Are they so ignorant that they don't know an underfed child without health care will grow up to be someone like me? It shouldn't take a college degree to figure out that you will require more services as an adult if your needs were ignored in childhood. Society needs to call it what it is—death on the installment plan. High premiums and low percentages. (The median life span for a Native American is 45 years.)

Whenever a medical problem occurs, I try various methods of treatment. The list is as long as what ails me, from "traditional" treatments to "experimental." Some of the medicines and procedures prescribed for me is not FDA approved. This is allowed, while other things that might be tried for muscle wasting and pain such as marijuana, are illegal. In an effort to find relief, I've tried Pow-Wows, acupuncture, meditation, wailing with the wolves, numerous herbs, Healing Circles, massage therapy, Holistic Healers, trigger injections (a combination of lidocaine, Novocain, and cortisone injected into the muscle spasms in my skull, neck, and shoulders), Wicca, three tattoos—a wolf (canis lupus), on my left forearm, a Celtic knot on my right wrist and a dream catcher around my ankle.

My first tattoo was done when I reached the age of 50. I dreamed what each tattoo should be and when it should be done. Doctors aren't impressed by my body art. This does not surprise me. A lot of people don't understand the significance of this art form. The tattoo artist who did each tattoo is a daughter-in-law. She protected me against infection and other problems that might occur. Everyone should visualize her own bottom line for surviving.

Reading the medical treatments my family used might give a clearer understanding of my attitude toward trying different things. If you stepped on a nail, you greased it and placed it over the doorway. If any evil Spirits came in, they would slip back out. This protected you from infection. My mother was protected from getting whooping cough because her parents had a black stallion blow its breath in her face. The treatment doctors suggested to keep my tapeworm at bay was kerosene or turpentine mixed with a tablespoon full of sugar. (I have no idea what long term poisoning this did to my system.) You stopped the sting of a bee by using the dirt from under an apple tree as a poultice. Your own urine was used to treat an earache as was cigarette smoke blown in the ear. Camphorated oil was also a remedy; it has now been taken off the market. The FDA said people were mistaking it for castor oil, drinking it and getting poisoned. This fall I made a batch of it for my family. A cousin--who also shared other remedies I had forgotten--gave the recipe to me. (She has multiple sclerosis; her sister has systemic lupus.) The oil has many uses: from treating swollen glands and joints to chest colds. You heat unsalted pork fat in camphorated oil and tie it around your neck. Leave it on overnight and it will draw out the congestion.

Some of the older ones say the stems of marijuana soaked in rubbing alcohol will work for joint pain. Though it is widely known that different forms of marijuana can be used for pain control and weight gain, very few doctors will prescribe it. The government grows marijuana for a select few in an ongoing drug trial. When these people die, the government will stop growing it, and the experiment will be considered finished.

Making marijuana illegal doesn't solve the problem though. Too often drugs and alcohol cause more pain than they relieve by contributing to ongoing poverty and disease. I say this like some backslapping, hand shaking, statistic seeker. Maybe I say it because I feel it's expected of me. It is truth and tragedy smeared likes clay on an unbaked pot. My truth doesn't involve pointing the middle finger of blame at anyone. Some of us try to overcome the environmental poisoning. Others find no peace except that of a momentary nature followed by a lifetime of payback.

"Slammin", "Huffin" and "Champagne" are names that whisper and scream the word addiction and despair. Just writing about these deadly "highs," I fear someone will try something new she might not have heard about before. A "sister" described to me the practice of "Slammin". I had asked her why I saw so many empty quart beer bottles lying around the reservation. (It is illegal to sell alcohol on a reservation. Reservations still have more overseers than the largest plantation ever had.) She said beer was injected into the veins of the nose and neck for a quick high by the younger ones. Many Native Americans are diabetic. Needles are borrowed from diabetic relatives and replaced without the owner's knowledge. AIDS is spreading because of this practice.

"Huffin". Inhaling substances from a paper or plastic bag to get high. If you see a young one with paint around her mouth, you will know the evil name of her poison. The names of other inhalants are too numerous to mention. Too numerous, and too dangerous to risk the responsibility of writing down their names.

"Champagne". A drink like none other. A bottle of household cleaner, cleaning fluid or a similar item is used. The higher the alcohol content the better the binge. The damage this does to the liver, kidneys, etc. can only be imagined. The consumption, and desire for this liquor, fills the eyes with unceasing tears.

Whether our health has been damaged by the poisons that have contaminated the air, land, and water or by our need to find an escape from the pain of daily life, we are all searching for a way to survive. These are my thoughts on getting by medically. Some illegal things I hesitated writing about. But what is the state going to do? Give me another illness? Get in line.

The most important piece of advice I can offer is don't be afraid of questioning your medical treatment. Don't allow anyone to blow off your questions. If it's bothering you, it's worth having an easily understood answer. When medical personnel stand up—the international signal to "hit the bricks"—stay seated. It's your life. It's their job. If they whip out their big words like some pervert in the park, don't sit there feeling ashamed and exposed. Ask that words be used that you do know.

Do your own investigation of any diagnosis or treatment. When you are given a prescription look up its use and side effects in a pill book. If you can't afford to buy one, page through the ones they keep at the pharmacy counter. Medical information can also be found at the library. Discuss your prescriptions with the pharmacist. Double-check her/his answer with another pharmacist who didn't fill your prescription. Get all of your medicines at one pharmacy so an ongoing record of what you are taking is kept. It will lessen the chance of getting something that might conflict with another drug you are already using.

During the writing of this article I have been having a "lupus flare." The amount of steroids I am taking has been raised three times. The pain medicine has also been doubled. A drug that is used for leprosy, pneumocystis pneumonia, and lupus was started. I'm trying Plaquenil because the steroids aren't healing the "lupus lesions" covering my body. My joints are so painful that the thought of placing my fingers on the keyboard is enough to keep the words piling up like snowflakes for days at a time. Something is also happening to the conncctive tissue between my ribs. It feels like my ribs are crushing together when I sit down at the computer. I feel the need to tell you what I am experiencing because it's as big a part of this article as the words are.

Equally important are some of the medicines I am taking: Plaquenil, Flecainide, Klonopin, Percocet, Macrodantin, prednisone, Tylenol, Dapsone, Flonase, Clobetasol Propionate, Fluori-Methane spray, Vicon Forte, 50,000 units Vitamin D weekly, Miacalcin Nasal spray, Muro 128, Patanol, Mycelex, Prevacid, lasix.

Today, Sue, came home from work to drive me to the neurologist. She knew the pain was so out of control that I wouldn't be able to express my medical needs. This doctor said the problem was the systemic lupus, not multiple sclerosis, and I should call the other doctor.

I waited until the next day to call the other specialist. The rheumatologist agrees that what "we" are trying isn't working. He told me to double the amount of steroids again, and gave me a schedule to follow. Each time the steroids are lowered my autoimmune system rebels with a vengeance. This is the fourth schedule change within two months. I remind him of this. We also discuss the 60 pounds I've lost. Neither of us knows when, or if, the wasting will stop. He is very kind when he tells me that during my next visit we need to discuss the use of IV Cytoxan. This is one of the chemotherapies. It is an experimental medicine used to try to put systemic lupus into remission. He explains that it will be a two-year program. I'm also very calm and kind during our discussion.

After talking to the doctor, I call Sue and tell her about the latest treatment that is being considered. The silence between us smothers and covers the dreaded word chemotherapy. This conversation has to wait until we are close enough to touch each other while we are talking. After twenty-two years together we can't bear not sharing everything. If there was a way to protect her from this I might try. But, no, she and me are we. During the phone silence she too heard the thud of me striking that place far below the bottom line.

CARD CARRYING MEMBER OF MEDICAID

I am the canary in the mine. My throat is hoarse from trying to warn others that their health insurance is in imminent jeopardy. The powers that be have found they can save countless amounts of money denying health care to others.

Many companies already feel no need to offer medical coverage and sick leave as employment benefits. The depth of people's desperation concerning their health care is enormous. Corporations have found that employees are willing to pay even more of their premiums to keep the barest of coverage in force. They can gauge just how tight to squeeze by watching what the government has done to Medicaid and Medicare recipients. There has been almost no out cry as healthcare money is decreased and diverted to other programs.

The fear of being turned away by doctors and hospitals when you are at one of the most vulnerable points in your life allows these unspeakable acts to be set in motion. Don't wait until you are closed in a state-controlled cage to do something. Fight against these despicable actions while there is still time. Don't waste your words misjudging women like me—those too disabled to work-- who have no other option for obtaining healthcare. I am not devaluing your paycheck with my myriad of illnesses. Blame the pharmaceuticals, doctors, hospitals and everyone else who is reaping huge profits from the suffering of others. Many of us know that our government would rather bomb people, in other countries, than spend money on the most helpless in this country.

I use the word Medicaid to describe my "insurance" coverage even though it is technically an M.C.O. A number of states now use the initials, M.C.O. (Managed Care Organization.) to represent this same service. These letters presumably lull you into thinking that they are akin to an H.M.O. or a P.P.O. They all basically blend into alphabet soup that leaves little to stick to your ribs except the illnesses you are trying to have treated.

Maryland is one of the states that opted for this form of

coverage. I fought for a year to try to get the state to fix the problems in the medical system that already existed. Yes, there were problems, but none that couldn't be fixed at a cheaper price. Revamping the entire system was something that benefited those who didn't need the states so called "entitlement" help anyway.

When the new plan—amusingly called "Health Choice" by Maryland-- was implemented, you were required to pick an M.C.O. you thought you would like to belong to. The M.C.O's were not allowed to solicit our business. We had no basis on which to make our decision. Our choice was comparable to drawing a name out of a paper bag. Hopefully your pick was one of the ones that offered a decent choice. Unless you knew someone who had experience with the few carriers offered, your only hope was that your pick was a livable one. We're talking about something as important as our health, but what it amounts to is the luck of the draw.

On the previous year's enrollment date, you are permitted to change to one of the other M.C.O.'s if you are dissatisfied. (Make sure to save your bag—those things cost money.) Each year you are mailed a paper with a list of insurance names. It's the absolute blind date of medical care. Some of my previous choices would have been easier to take if I had put the brown bag over my head.

Last year I wanted to change plans but because our area postal system was contaminated with anthrax, my papers did not arrive. When my partner called the state she was told that it was up to me to prove that I hadn't received the packet. The only way to prove it was if the postal service returned the packet to the state. No one, including the state was getting mail, but that was of no consequence. I had no choice but to limp along for another year with less than satisfactory coverage.

This was truly a hardship because I am under the Special Populations section of Maryland Medicaid due to a number of incurable illnesses. These illnesses require seeing different specialists. This presents a problem because many specialists do not want to deal with Medicaid or the mountain of paperwork the government heaps on them. A number of doctors have told me that they either not participate in the program or spend extra money to hire someone to handle the paperwork. If you wanted a system to collapse under its own mismanagement, this is how you would go about arranging it.

You are not allowed to have any of the books that explain what the insurance covers to make an informed choice. The doctors, hospitals, pharmacies, and specialists that take part in each plan remain a mystery until you are enrolled. Through the years I have been enrolled in this "system" I have learned to lower my expectations.

Everyone is required to choose a primary care doctor who will be in charge of decision making. Hopefully, you will find someone who is compassionate and willing to send you to a specialist when needed.

Don't expect to find the address or phone number of numerous providers in your book. Many times you will find doctors listed who do not accept your plan. When you phone their office it helps if you've developed a thick skin. Numerous people, including office personnel, feel that those who need the states help must also be lawbreakers.

When Medicaid was first changed incentives were offered to get primary care doctors to enroll in the program. (At the beginning of the year a lump sum of money is paid per patient.) In the past—presumably—box seats to sporting events, cruises, tickets to plays, expensive meals, etc., were given to entice the doctor to rein in the cost of the treatment that was offered to patients. If you have an ailment that requires frequent monitoring, this cuts into the insurance carriers and doctors' "profit." It creates an atmosphere that you might not receive adequate care for incurable illnesses that require a lot of time and treatment. You are not always given options, concerning your health, if they are costly. Prescriptions, and other profit reducing treatments, are not as readily supplied as they once were.

You need a referral by your primary doctor to see a specialist, to receive diagnostic testing or have a surgical procedure. (The doctor then has to have the approval of the health plan before issuing the referral. Her training is not enough to make a sensible decision while you are in the office.) I have learned to go through the yellow pages of the phone book and locate the address and phone number for myself. It's the least frustrating plan of action. This way you can hope to find someone that you've had experience with and ask your doctor to refer you to them. It also saves the doctor's staff work in locating the necessary information required to fill out each referral request for the M.C.O. They get the final say in how many visits you are allowed and what else they feel is necessary. "You Will Not Be Seen By A Medical Person without This Referral!" Just look around the office and you will see it written in various languages, taped on numerous walls.

A few exceptions that do not require a referral are a mammogram and a Pap smear. You may also go to the emergency room if it's deemed that it's truly an emergency. "If you think you need emergency care (see the section "Emergency Care"), call 911 or go to the nearest emergency room right away." Hope that your injury isn't a neurological one, and that you can remember where your book is, and what it said to do.

There are a few examples of what constitutes emergencies: "An emergency is when not seeing a doctor right away to get care could result in death or very serious bodily harm. The problem is so severe that someone with an average knowledge of health can tell the problem may be life threatening or cause serious damage to your body." Severe bleeding, chest pain, loss of consciousness, very bad bleeding, very bad burns, shakes called convulsions or seizures."

You are supposed to call your doctor before going to the emergency room. She, or a replacement, should be available on a 24-hour basis. "You may also call our Nurse HelpLine 24 hours a day, 7 days a week for help." This judgment can also be made by someone who has no medical training. If you do get to talk to a nurse their priority appears to be having you wait until the doctor is back in her office. If I feel that my health is in jeopardy I dispense with all of the above and let the hospital sort out whose authority I have trampled. What are they going to do? Give me another illness? In this day and time that is not as unlikely as it once was, but I'm not going to play a guessing game when I believe that my life is in jeopardy. Why should my wheelchair receive better maintenance than I do?

If I were truly a canary I would have flown out of various emergency rooms and doctor's offices. Only the absolute need of my medical health kept me lying on the stretcher. I've witnessed my file being tossed back and forth because the doctors in the ER did not want to treat someone with so many health problems. I've listened with total shame while the list of my illnesses was read aloud for everyone to hear. At a new specialist's office I heard him scream at his nurse about making an appointment for me. He said, "How in the hell am I going to get her out of here in five minutes with all of the problems she has?"

As a feminist I am ashamed to write these things and tell you that I was silent. Silent because I was afraid of not receiving the treatment I needed without delay. If I couldn't speak up how can I hope that others will? I won't blame it on multiple sclerosis, systemic lupus, osteoporosis that has caused me to break each of my ankles twice, heart, kidney and other diseases. Perhaps the overwhelming pain caused me to hope that someone would at least be humane enough to ease what hurt—if only temporarily. I gave up on cures a long time ago, but I still want to enjoy what's left of my life with my partner of twenty-seven years.

Be your own canary in the mine. Make a shrill noise that no one can ignore. If we all refuse to be treated in this manner maybe it will give hope that the medical system as we now know it will change. Women who are receiving state aid cannot do it alone. We need the help of our more fortunate sisters.

Let your legislators know by phone, email, fax, letter writing and your vote that you will not tolerate this ongoing disassembly of the medical safety net for the poor and disabled. In an election year what you do can truly make a difference.

TEAR DOWN THIS WALL!

When Ronald Reagan said, "Tear down this Wall," his quote was met with applause worldwide. He was speaking about the wall between East and West Berlin.

Today a 1,900 mile wall is being built in the southwestern United States. This wall is being built, with support by many, to keep immigrants out. It also effectively stops local American Indians from traveling freely to visit family members as was always the custom.

A third wall remains basically invisible. It's the barrier that keeps us from truthfully speaking our mind on numerous issues. The one where openly practicing our customs and ways of life cause others to become silent or react angrily. Sometimes we are told that fishing, hunting, eating various forms of wild meat, using guns, knives, bows, etc. is no longer needed because there are stores where food can be bought. Other times it's said that these practices are okay for 'us' because it's 'our' culture. These beliefs leave the impression that we get special privileges because to do otherwise would be discriminatory. Or, that we are somehow so childlike that we need to be told what is deemed proper. This third reason also exists because not everyone has access to plentiful money, and our way of life ensures food is available and can be used to help others.

I've always resisted allowing others to define what my way of life should be, or worse, granting me the "privilege" to eat wild game and fish because it is my culture. Eating food that has been filled with growth hormones and antibiotics does not appeal to me. I don't need anyone's permission to hunt, fish, or grow whatever food that I've always been accustomed to having in my diet.

When animal rights activists started going into the woods and making loud noises to scare away the game, it temporarily frightened family members. Never mind that we have every right to practice our way of life. I tell others to contact a game warden and make her do her job. Hunting is legal, and personal beliefs do not entitle anyone to interfere with another's rights.

Frequently you see deer carcasses lying alongside the road after being hit by a car. People are constantly being injured in these accidents also because there are fewer hunters to keep the herds culled. There's also too little space available for wildlife to graze freely because of the building boom taking place everywhere. Many times I see on the news frantic deer crashing through store windows because they mistake their shadows or those of trees for an open space.

These things are inhumane according to us. We do not take the life of an animal lightly. We give thanks for the life they have given to feed us. The meat is divided between the elderly, handicapped, poor and then amongst family members and friends.

How someone is culturally raised does not equate special status or privilege. The opposite is true. Our way of life has been the norm, for many of us, for centuries. For certain populations to decide that it is somehow wrong unless you are from a certain race of people is beyond condescending. It's wrong for countless reasons.

The time for honest conversation on all sides is long overdue. I'm weary of explaining my way of life, and being made to feel that I'm being patronized at best and tolerated and tokenized at worst. I'm not the only one who has remained silent in fear of losing friends, movement workers and other "equals." It's hundreds of years late to kick the door off the closet—hinges and all-- that holds all tribes of American Indians in last place. Instead of First Nation we are referred to as "other" on numerous written forms, and in the hearts and minds of others, while we statistically fill the space of almost every area of deprivation documented in this country.

Debating the massive failings that continue to take place is akin to hollering "Queer" in someone's place of worship. Anger replaces dialogue in the majority of instances and the chance for a totally honest discussion is once again lost.

Since the age of five I knew that my place in life belonged with other two spirit women. This fact had to be obvious to adults, but no one ever questioned the way I dressed or did anything else that was usually classified as male. I've been with my partner, Sue, for over thirty-one years. She is white, and comes from a middle class background. Her education includes a university degree. I was one of the first in my large family to graduate high school. Sue tells me that her class privilege accounts for her ability to gain the status and recognition she has received. It allows her to work in white collar jobs that pay well and offer numerous benefits. We have countless debates about education and class. Her view of degrees is that they are basically bullshit. That anyone who knows how to look up information, and has tuition money, can be admitted. I believe she is wrong, and view these degrees with great respect. If they weren't so important why would they often be the first question that comes up when meeting others? There are two main questions at most gatherings. Where did you attend school? (I've learned they don't mean high school.) And, where do you work? No one has ever been impressed by my education except my family. Working at a textile factory or a cook at a truck stop has received the same wide-eyed look. Not one of awe, but because I don't beat around the bush when telling the hard truth. Throughout the years I've developed a number of handicaps, and I now get a pass on answering work related history.

We've both received awards for community service over the years, and Sue was also an appointed Human Relations Commissioner. I've won two Superior court cases concerning child welfare. These cases were fought due to the unfair treatment of my children. They will benefit children everywhere because of my determination.

We agreed early on that while I wouldn't give up any of my cultural ways, Sue decided what she wanted to freely take part in. She was interested in fishing, camping and learning the ways of all types of wild animals. I've gained many forms of education of white middle class life from going to the theater, foreign films and museums of all types, and from the love and use of computers. Everything can equal out if there is trust and open, truthful dialogue.

Twice, during our long time relationship, Sue's job canceled my health insurance as her partner. Both times they switched to companies that didn't have partnership benefits. She quit her job the first time it happened, and is putting out resumes as I write because it has recently happened again. She is livid because she feels the sharp blade of discrimination personally. I understand what Sue is saying, but it has been a way of life since birth in all aspects of my life. There are only so many battles that I can fight at any given times.

Every time I tell the medical community that I'm insured under Medicaid their demeanor automatically changes. That old look of 'we're about to have our pockets picked' gets replaced by a sour expression of 'We thought we were going to gouge a real insurance.'

Damned right it hurts when you are treated like a third class citizen, but we will get through this new battle. As long as we continue to fight as partners in prejudice, this country will not divide us because of our sexual identity.

We raised my three sons and are now helping the four grandchildren. Our granddaughter will graduate this year, and the first grandson graduated last year. Another granddaughter is in eighth grade and the youngest grandson is in third grade. The three sons graduated high school and are working in union jobs. Their income is higher, and all have more benefits than our generation was ever able to achieve. Our battle to overcome the type of starvation level poverty the Appalachians created is well known by most. Menial labor, little chance for higher education and a generous helping of genetically engineered illnesses has destroyed countless lives. The same situation is true all over this land for the majority of my people. It's past time others recognize us more often than just when certain holidays arrive.

I have worked to encourage my family to strive for a higher education. Each generation needs to surpass the former one.

No doubt joining the women's movement was the ultimate way to learn about class, culture and discrimination at warp speed. When I became involved in movement work it amazed me that so many feminists were impoverished. I based this on the way everyone dressed. It never occurred to me they were "dressing down" because it was their idea of how to show we were all equal. Just when I could afford decent clothes, society up and changed the rules again!

In 1976—America's Bicentennial—I was one of the co-coordinators of a 55 day picket in front of the White House. NOW was the sponsor for the event. It was a reenactment of the early suffragettes. We protested for the E.R.A.-Equal Rights Amendment-twelve hours a day in four hour shifts. Women from around the country came to help participate in the event.

I worked continuously during the 55 days as well as and for months leading up to it. I helped making all of the necessary banners and pamphlets and meeting to figure out how we would fill all of the days with other protestors. It was never taken into consideration that I had three young children. The fact that I was the only one who was a mother was never mentioned. The E.R.A. was the only thing that was of importance. Looking back I feel deep shame that I was so blinded by suddenly being "included" in something so important.

Another lesson I learned was watching how a small clique would decide that certain members weren't acceptable. The "untouchables" would be given the silent treatment whenever their ideas were suggested to the group. This ugly incident took place a number of times, and the ones taking the abuse would stop coming. I'm sure that my race protected me from this type of behavior; I've never been accused of keeping a low profile. I'd never viewed this dynamic before among adults. It took a number of years until I understood how this process was a conscious way of life in many groups.

During this same time period American Indians, from various tribes, were walking to Washington from California. This was our time to protest countless broken treaties, and acts of outright discrimination and evilness. The place of protest was also in front of the White House.

When the ERA protest was being planned it was decided that long white dresses and large white hats would be worn. Parasols were also to be carried. Everyone agreed on the details except me. This was not my style of dress nor had it ever been. Despite others' arguments to the contrary, I said I'd be dressed in t-shirt and jeans, and my long hair would be in its usual braid.

On July 5th, 1976 the protests began. When I was dropped off at the place of picketing, I heard loud drumming and chanting. "What the fuck!" My so called co-coordinators ran up to me and said,

"Judith, they're 'your' people and you have to do something. Those people are armed with various weapons, and we don't know what will happen!" Excuse me? What happened to we're all equals and me busting my ass working to help pass the ERA? My mind was reeling. Something was totally out of whack. I asked what type of weapons they were talking about. "You know—knives, axes, hatchets, weapons!" Through clenched teeth I said, "Those are not weapons. They are items used for camping and living off the land. Not everyone can afford a hotel."

As I turned away the words being chanted came through loud and clear. As the drums were being hit the words kept tempo. "Bitches with Riches getting more Rights for Whites." A number of clichés came to mind, but the better part of me won out. The situation was too serious and heartbreaking.

Thankfully, I saw a friend, and started my long walk across the White House front. Chief Turkey Tayac from the Piscataway tribe was leaning against the wrought iron fence. He was in his eighties at that time. When I reached him he put both hands on either side of my face and said, "Look at those beautiful Cherokee cheekbones. Why should she be looking so sad?" I explained what "our" group was protesting about. As I spoke numerous brothers and sister's circled around us and listened to what I was saying about equal rights. The drumming and chanting stopped. Everyone agreed that we were all there for the same purpose, but why hadn't anyone come over earlier to discuss the same thing? (Good question, Judith, and how have you survived so many years with your head buried dirt deep.) I offered to do anything needed to help with the other protest. Print flyers; arrange places to stay at campuses, etc. My personal experience learning what it meant to work both sides of the street. Needless to say no one apologized or gave a thought to the outrageous act of discrimination they had perpetrated.

We wore buttons so others would know where to seek help in case of trouble. More than once I was called an "elitist" by other NOW members. Right, I'm the one who yanked several white women to the pavement when the bullets started whizzing by us, and they wanted to see what was happening. (Gun ignorance.) A man climbed over the fence and Secret Service agents came out from behind every bush and killed him. The police required us to stay in place until we could be questioned about the incident. Helen Thomas was the first reporter to appear. When I asked I could respond to her questions, a Secret Service agent informed me, "You're a liberated woman. You can say whatever you want."

Another time a Vietnam vet dumped out his duffle bag in search of a knife. He was screaming that we were communist whores and the reason he couldn't find a job. "Judith, you're the coordinator. You better alert the Secret Service." (I still have the "Elitist" button to remind me of just how far I've come.)

When the 55 day protest was over there was a large rally with several speakers of note. The other coordinators all had their own speeches to give throughout the event. I was given a number of telegrams to read from "dignitaries" who couldn't come to the grand finale. By that time there must have been at least twenty or thirty people remaining. Thank the powers that be for the friends who stood by me.

A month after this successful event was over I was asked to help organize another protest. I'd worked my rear end off, and it was assumed that I'd help organize another event. I'm a people person, and had no problem recruiting numerous other women to join the movement. When I said I'd spent too much time away from my young children, and it was time to take a rest, I received the same treatment that was doled out to the other women who became *persona non gratis*.

Paybacks are hell, and I apologize to no one for laughing heartily when I heard the leader of the clique had finally overstepped her bounds, and was no longer welcome anywhere.

Our silence has never solved the inequalities that exist in our movement, and perhaps the truth won't set us entirely free. However, tearing down this wall of unspoken prejudices and unexpressed attitudes will surely be the best starting place for others with an open mind to wrap their words around.

THE TEXTILE FACTORY

This year was the 102nd anniversary of the Triangle Shirtwaist Factory fire in New York City. The event occurred on March 25, 1911, and 146 lives were lost because of fire employees jumped to their deaths from the 8th and 9th floors. The owners were on the 10th floor and jumped from one building to another to escape the blaze. It was said the fire was ignited by one of them dropping a lit cigar. Valuable time was lost because they didn't tell the workers there was a fire.

The overwhelming majority of those who died were Jewish and Italian immigrant women. Their ages ranged from 48 years to two fourteen year old girls. The workers were mainly women who worked long hours with few breaks allowed. The escalation of the fire was reported to be from locked exit and stairway doors by managers to force long workdays. (This contributed directly to the requirement for exit signs to be prominently located.)

The fire led to worker safety laws, and the specific beginning of the ILGWU-The International Ladies Garment Workers Union.

The ILGWU was the union I belonged to in the 60's. Despite many beneficial union laws to protect workers, the behavior of others will always be a problem when rules are violated. Due to just such an incident I wrote the following story.

After graduating high school in 1962, I went to work at one of the local factories. The fact that I was seventeen didn't deter the ones in charge from hiring someone underage. My mother, sister, and two aunts were also employed at this textile factory. It was the natural progression for many female family members entering the workforce.

Anyone who ever worked in one of these sweatshops can attest to its mind-numbing, back-breaking nature. The noise, fiber dust, stale air, and nonstop pressure to work faster on assembly lines was intense. In truth, it was pure unabated hell. The knowledge of what working there meant was of no consequence. It was meant to be a means of survival, until something better came along. Something better rarely, if ever, came into your life. Once you became used to the grueling atmosphere your dreams were replaced by the reality of survival.

During my two years of work at the sportswear factory, I witnessed two women suffer a mental breakdown. Their screams made the hair on the back of your neck stand up. Other women would carry the woman out, and hardly a moment of work would be lost. Slowing down might allow the Spirits to catch you next, or the bosses would find a way to get rid of someone else who wasn't producing to their satisfaction. It was a hellish place for a naive teenager.

Men held the positions of authority. (Throughout life I've learned this is the rule rather than the exception.) As a teenager, I was ill equipped to deal with these men. At that time there was no term for sexual harassment. The word "fresh" was meant to cover all forms of abuse. It was accepted as the way things were, and you remained silent to protect your job and reputation.

When one of the line supervisors started harassing me I was shocked. He was old enough to be my father. I was worried that even with the noise of the sewing machines, and cutting equipment the women would hear what he was saying, and believe I had done something to encourage his advances.

I thought if I worked even harder he would see that I was someone worthy of respect. Needless to say it gave him permission to embolden his tactics.

There was a union at our workplace, and I decided to file a grievance when nothing I did failed to stop his constant, unwanted behavior.

I learned at the meetings I attended to report any abuse to the unions. Two of my aunts were officers in our local chapter of the ILGWU. They were president and vice president.

When I told them what was taking place they were outraged. I was too embarrassed to tell them everything, but they knew me as a person who would not lie.

They went to management with what I told them, and total chaos ensued! These were two women who wouldn't back down from anything. The fact that the victim was a young family member fueled their anger.

An earlier sit-down strike at the factory over another issue had been successful, and I'm sure the shop knew my aunts wouldn't hesitate to call a strike over this cause.

The man who harassed me tried to say I was lying. When that tactic didn't work he tried to convince me that I misunderstood what he was repeatedly suggesting. With my aunts' strength and backing I refused to allow his intimidation to continue. It was a frightening time in my life.

The ones in charge at the sportswear factory held a closed meeting and agreed that he would be fired immediately, and no time would be lost because of a strike. The matter was settled without further action, because time was always more important than a workers of any rank.

My aunts, two usually fun loving women, found nothing humorous in the disrespectful way their niece was treated. I was apparently the only one surprised at the outcome, and amazed that management took what occurred seriously. The steadfast backing of my aunts and the strength of the union assured the outcome.

They were feminists before the term was known or understood. Credit goes to my aunts for teaching me how to fight and win when someone makes you feel uncomfortable, and you believe the behavior is wrong. This incident was no doubt one of the earliest examples of sexual harassment.

The memory of that incident has forever remained with me. It taught me to speak up for others who might not have gained a voice. Young or old, we need others to believe us and stand together. Reaching other women through the written word has promoted and expedited numerous laws and knowledge of wrongs that would otherwise go uncorrected.

Years later I saw my harasser. He was parking cars in a small town. His actions cost him a high paying job, and no doubt taught him a lesson that will remain with him forever.

This incident taught me a valuable lesson. Remaining silent does not protect you or anyone else. Even if there is failure in the beginning, strength in numbers will undoubtedly result in success for the greater good of many. The rights of others often begins with the fight for justice for one. Herstory is filled with countless stories that supports this dynamic.

There is a renewed battle taking place to dismantle unions around our country. Without the power of unions behind workers to insure that safety and legal rights are insured, there will be a lack of adherence to rules that protect those doing the work. One only needs to look at what happens in large accidents to see what happens when there is a break down in safety standards. This constant fear of loss of life exists in all aspects of the workforce. Without union supervision the loss will return to the sub-standards of previous times.

MIKE MEETS THE DYKES

We had just finished eating dinner when the first call came in. My family numbers many so we are used to receiving phone calls on various subjects. Sometimes it's burdensome; other times it's rewarding.

The call we received that summer night was from one of my younger sisters. She usually keeps her life private, but this night she was asking for help in whispered tones. Before she could finish telling me what had happened, I heard her boyfriend, Mike, demand that she hang up the friggin' phone.

When I hung up I told Sue and our sons about the conversation. We discussed whether we should go over to her apartment or wait for her to call again. Her boyfriend has a serious drinking problem. Like many with this addiction, he becomes abusive after enough alcohol coats his cowardice.

Before the dinner dishes were washed, the phone rang again. It was my sister and she was still whispering. Not because her boyfriend might overhear her talking, but because he had choked her, damaging her vocal cords. Her three littlest ones were crying in the background. To gain time to think, I asked to speak to her teenage son. He told me that Mike had "gone off" and hurt his mother. He was told to barricade the apartment door and not let that man back inside. I assured him that we'd be there shortly.

Sue and I with two of the boys drove to my sister's apartment. We could see a struggle had taken place. I asked where the children were. Three little heads came up from behind the living room couch where they were hiding. "Hi Aunt Judy. Hi, Aunt Sue," they said. The relief that showed on their faces fueled our rage. I asked where Mike was. "He's probably at one of the bars where he hangs out," she said. We nodded, and handed her a baseball bat to use for protection.

After leaving my sister and her kids, we started cruising the parking lots of neighborhood dives. At the second bar we saw Mike's pickup truck parked in the middle of the lot. Adrenaline started seeping out of every one of my pores. Our one piece of luck was finding an empty parking space next to his truck. Sue pulled into the slot and turned off the ignition.

We discussed disabling his vehicle so he couldn't get away before we "chatted" him up. Our first idea was to remove the distributor cap. On closer inspection we noted that the hood of his truck was chained and padlocked. Those two items had to be worth more than his entire vehicle.

With that plan thwarted we decided to flatten one of the tires. Sue asked if I had my pocketknife with me. My knife is like that credit card commercial--I don't leave home without it. I handed her the knife.

She quietly opened the car door and leaned down beside his truck. Without missing a beat she stuck the knife blade in up to the handle. I'd never tried this before and didn't have a clue as to whether the tire would explode or what else might unexpectedly occur. The unknown, and a few health problems, kept me inside the car. Someone needed to be the lookout.

Cutting the tire went so smoothly that we decided to puncture another one. This gave us insurance in case he had a spare tire. We wanted to slow his chance of following us if we were observed. Sue said, "I'm cutting the tire high up on the whitewall so it can't be fixed." Nice touch! How do I love thee? Let me count the ways, my woman.

Now what? It was tempting to leave, but there was our entire family member's back at the apartment counting on us. We walked slowly to the front of the bar. It was decided that Sue and Steve would go inside and tell Mike's cronies what kind of a friend they had. Marky and I would wait outside as lookouts. Marky was too young to even go in bars and we didn't want him to witness any violence that might occur.

We peered inside the darkened glass front door and spotted him right away. He was seated on a stool in the foyer talking on the pay phone. The length of the bar could be seen through the doorway behind him. Sue pulled the door open, and as she did we heard him threatening to hurt my sister and the children again.

From there on it was like watching a surreal movie. Sue looked like she was walking in slow motion as she crossed the floor in three long strides. She wrapped both of her hands around Mike's throat. The phone dropped. I watched it swing back and forth like a pendulum. Sue beat his head against the plate glass window without loosening her grip on his neck. With each head bang she said, "How do you like it? How do you like it?" His tongue had little trouble touching the bottom of his chin. His eyes looked like twin eight balls racked.

The thought that she might kill him was a serious one. I'd never seen her like this. My plan of staying outside ended. I couldn't allow her to get into trouble because of him. When I loosened her hold he was barely able to stand.

A woman who was tending bar came out and announced that she had called the police. I told her what had inspired the incident. She didn't care. We were to leave. His compadres continued their drinking.

The pause gave Mike enough time to catch his breath, and regain his boozy bravado. He started making threats about what he was going to do. He had nearly been killed, and yet he still acted like he had won.

Without a thought I walked over and stuck my forefinger in under his sternum. I said, "I'm going to cut your fucking heart out. Your days of tormenting my sister and her children are over." He thought my finger was a knife, and his life had to flash before him for a second time. Meanwhile, the bartender was parroting "The police are on their way, the police are on their way."

Steve, who was sixteen, wanted to drag him outside. His anger at the damage that this man had done was understandable. We had raised him and his brothers to respect women.

To add to the moment, my sister had stayed on the phone listening to what was happening. Amidst the chaos no one had bothered to hang up the phone dangling by its cord.

True to the barmaid's word she had called the cops. We heard a faint wail of sirens. "Time to go," I said. We exited the bar and ran to our car. As we were pulling out the police drove by us and parked in the spot we had vacated. We waved at the officers like the good law abiding citizens that we were.

That night, while we were reviewing the bar scene with my sister, Mike called. I told him to come pack up his crap and vacate the apartment. He had the audacity to accuse us of slicing his tires, and threatened to press charges. I suggested a convenient place he could stick any legal papers.

I wish I could say that it was the end of his presence in my sister's life. He made another appearance six months later--insisting that he was moving back. She had her oldest son call us while she kept him busy.

We arrived and escorted him and his belongings outside. I waited in the open doorway to make sure he left. He swaggered to his truck and pulled a .12 gauge shotgun out of the gun rack. If he was dumb enough to try and shoot me, I figured I could fall backwards into the apartment before he could get a shot off. He laid the gun in the front seat beside him. Big tough man! As someone who has always owned a gun or two I was unimpressed by his bravado. Only a fool would carry a loaded gun around. Whenever I talk about weapons with Sue, and my disgust at what people do with them, she always looks at me with a knowing look.

One time she asked me since I felt the way I did why did I stay heavily armed? Damn, I thought she understood that they were just an extension of my femininity.

In the future I hope Mike remembers it was he who that kept showing up uninvited and the ensuing result. He needed a gun. The Dyke Disposal Unit only needed to hear the plea of a woman in trouble.

LONE FEATHER

The line leading to where the poet sat,
lagged with the slowest movement
imaginable. Time mattered naught.
Her signature was all that mattered.

She nodded serenely to everyone who
paid the price for a book full of her
words. Someone so gifted was worth
any price asked. Money was no object.

I shifted from one foot to foot another,
awaiting my turn at the metal table.
Discussing writing with her personally
was a treat I'd savor forever in thought.

When my turn finally arrived we
talked to each other like sisters.
She of the same culture spared
extra time for our conversation.

As we spoke I gave her a lone
turkey wing feather in respect.
It was offered to keep the wind
moving beneath the written words.

With the slightest movement she
slipped the feather onto her lap.
Was she afraid of offending
others not of our skin color?

Did this feeling of disbelief
slip silently past others in line?
How could respect accorded
the wild leave your world?

My once proud opinion hit reverse.
I handed the book to another admirer.
Why allow something inside my home
that couldn't be read without shame?

LOSIN' OUR ORIGIN

Religion is no longer
the opiate of the masses.
Opiates are the opiate
of choice for many, and
any little kid can opt
to buy crack cocaine.

So where's the hook to snag 'em with?

How do you control
someone when they are
too stoned to sting?
What can you replace
this quick-fix feeling
of satisfaction with?

So-sigh-ety searches for a new gaff.

"If you would just think
more positively your
life would be better.
Smile more. Expect less.
Life is crap because
your outlook created it."

Reservations rack and reel with this gem.

CHAOS

In the quiet
of the riot,
when the reason
trickles in.

When the heat
of hatred passes,
and the surge of
violence ends.

As the smoke
and ashes settle,
blotting out
the noonday sun.

Will we pause to
seek new answers
but maintain the
status quo again?

ACKNOWLEDGEMENTS

First I'd like to thank all the editors of anthologies and publications who chose me as one of their backup writers. Without the encouragement and confidence of those who published me, my words would never have been heard. In particular I thank Carol Anne Douglas who in 1981 with *off our backs* made me believe in my own value as a writer.

Next I'd like to thank all the women who reassured me that writers don't need perfect spelling and grammar--only editors do. And all those who treated me as an academic equal despite my lack of formal education. My hats off to Sue Lenaerts, Carol Anne Douglas, Jean Sirius, Susan Koppelman, Janet Mason, G.L. Morrison, Julia Penelope, Nancy Pfaff, Deb Friedman, Meredith Pond, Riggin Waugh, Suzanne Sunshower.

My gratitude also goes to the women's publications and presses, existing and bygone, that gave me a voice: *Quest: A Feminist Quarterly*, *Aegis Magazine*, *Sojourner: The Women's Forum*, *off our backs*, *On the Issues: The Progressive Woman's Quarterly*, *Mother Warriors Voice*, *Lesbian Health News*, *Quiet Mountain Essays* and to *Sinister Wisdom* for which I have served on the Board of Directors for over a decade.

And not least of all I want to recognize my family who provided so much of the material for my work: my precious parents, my beloved sisters and brothers, my three sons and their families and Sue, my life partner. And a special thanks to artist and daughter-in-law Andrea Witherow for the illustration of how she viewed me, "Strong Enough to Bend."

Previous publication of the work in this collection (in part):
"Strained Class Windows," *Sojourner: The Women's Forum*, 1994, and *Women's Health, Readings on Social, Political and Economic Issues*, edited by Nancy Worcester and Marianne H. Whatley, Kendall/Hunt, 1994 ;

"Go Yell It on the Mountain," *Woman's Work, Short Stories*, edited by Michelle Sewell, Girlchild Press, 2010; "Native American Mother," *Quest: A Feminist Quarterly*, 1977, and *Families in the U.S.: Kinship, and Domestic Politics*, edited by K.V. Hansen and A. Garey, Temple University Press, 1998 and *Gender Through the Prism of Difference*, edited by Maxine Baca Zinn, Pierette Hondegneu-Sotelo, Michael Messner, Allyn and Bacon, 2000; "Columbus Day Revisited," *MOM, Candid Memoirs by Lesbians about the First Woman in their Life*, edited by Nisa Donnelly, Alyson Publications, Inc., 1998; "Cardboard Coffin," *Sinister Wisdom #68/69*, 2006; "Are We There Yet," *Beginnings: Lesbians Talk About the First Time They Met Their Long-Term Partner*, edited by Lindsay Elder, Alyson Publications, Inc. 1998; "Not Just Merely Queer," *Queerly Classed*, edited by Susan Raffo, South End Press, March 1997; "Wailing With the Wolves," *Through the Eye of the Deer, An Anthology of Native American Women Writers*, edited by Carolyn Dunn and Carol Comfort, Aunt Lute Books, 1999; "Hello Walls," *off our backs*, May 1981; "Help, I've Fallen, and No One Has Even Noticed," *Woman's Studies, Health and Wellness*, edited by Sophie Harding, University of Calgary; 2004; "Group Therapy for the Uninitiated," *Lesbian Health News*, 2003 ; "Can You Feel the Pain," *Lesbian Health News*, 2004; "Don't Blame Me, I Voted For Myself," *On The Issues: The Progressive Woman's Quarterly*, 1997; "Yo' Done Bridge is Falling Down," *This Bridge Called My Home*, edited by Gloria Anzaldua and Analouise Keating, Routlege, Inc., 2002; "Card Carrying Member of Medicaid," *off our backs*, 2002; "The Textile Factory," *Back Off!* edited by Martha Langelan, Simon and Schuster, 1993; "Mike Meets the Dykes," *That Takes Ovaries! Bold Females and Their Brazen Acts*, edited by Rivka Solomon, Crown/Random House, 2002.

Photographs are credited to Sue Lenaerts, Deb Friedman, and Elizabeth Hart.

ABOUT THE AUTHOR

Judith K. Witherow is a poet, essayist and storyteller. A mixed blood Native American/Irish lesbian raised in rural Appalachian poverty, she writes about her life experiences with disability, gender, sexual orientation, race and class from a perspective influenced by her early heritage.

Judith describes the hunger and cold of being poor in America in brutally honest first person accounts. She suffered along with her five siblings and parents the effects of malnutrition and industrial poisoning as well as various problems with their small town neighbors.

Judith's attentions to feminist issues were always encapsulated by her greater understanding of class and race. Following the initial excitement of the women's movement was the disillusionment that newly won "rights" were for middle class women who wanted an equal arena with men. Very little has changed for women of her background.

Chronic pain and illness have shaped her recent life. But she is still sharing her stories with the world. Her four decades of storytelling reflect this spirit and offer a rare chance to hear the voices of otherwise silenced women. She remains politically active in various causes via her computer. The struggle to protect rights and work to seek justice for the disenfranchised continue to be her forever battles.

Judith's first book *All Things Wild: Poems from the Appalachians* was published in 2003. With her life partner Sue Lenaerts, Judith edited *Sinister Wisdom #68/69*, "Death, Grief and Surviving."

In 1994 she won the Audre Lorde First Annual Award for Non-fiction. She was awarded "Community Builder for Decades" by WPFW (Pacifica) Radio in 2007. She received an Award of Recognition from the Baltimore City Council, 2010.

Judith is online at http://www.jkwitherow.com.